Red Sky Anthology

Reading Out Loud in

Northern Michigan

Red Sky Series/Book 1

Randy Evans

Copyright © 2016 Little Traverse Press, Bay Harbor, Michigan

ISBN: 978-1-63491-121-4

All rights reserved. No part of this publication may be reproduced, stored in a retrieval system, or transmitted in any form or by any means, electronic, mechanical, recording or otherwise, without the prior written permission of the author.

Published by Little Traverse Press, Bay Harbor, Michigan

Printed on acid-free paper.

The characters and events in this book are fictitious. Any similarity to real persons, living or dead, is coincidental and not intended by the author.

Little Traverse Press
2016

First Edition

BLOG: randyevansauthor.com

FICTION/Literary<LITERARY COLLECTIONS/American/General<FAMILY RELATIONSHIPS/ Death/Grief/Bereavement/Spirituality/Healing/Breast/ Cancer/Patients

Selected pieces in this work were previously published in different form in the following: ProQuest LLC (2007), NPR This I Believe (2011), Bear River Review (2012), Petoskey News and Review (2014), Walloon Writers Review (2015).

Cover photograph by Mike Schlitt, Visions of Mike

*To my teacher,
Hollis Summers (1916-1987), Distinguished Professor
of Literature, Ohio University*

Also by Randy Evans

Out of the Inferno: A Husband's Passage through Cancerland (Red Sky Series/Book 2)

Crooked River: Love and Adventure in Northern Michigan (Red Sky Series/Book 3)

The Lawnmower Club: How Leo Zitzelberger Lost and Found Paradise on Earth (Red Sky Series/Book 4)

randyevansauthor.com

Contents

Preface ix

Poems 1
   November, Petoskey, Michigan 3
   Autumn Haiku 5
   Up North Cottage 6
   Autumn Chill 8
   October Crossing 10
   Greenway, Cotswolds 12
   Still Life 13
   Snow Plows in April 14
   Trillium 15
   Woman Before a Canvas 16
   Detroit Metro 17
   Fishing for Wind 18

Short Stories 23
   Big Little Hawk 25
   Mikage's Escape 29

One-Act Play 45
   Wanting to Be Liked 47

Fable 59
   Trella: Love Fable of an Oak Tree 61

Memoir (excerpt) 69
   Out of the Inferno: A Husband's Passage Through
      Cancerland 71

Novel (Excerpts) 129
   Crooked River: Love and Adventure in Northern
      Michigan 131

The Lawnmower Club: How Leo Zitzelberger Lost
and Found Paradise on Earth.................................... 183
ACKNOWLEDGEMENTS... 239
ABOUT THE AUTHOR 241

Preface

On the first Monday evening of each month, I park my car near the public library in downtown Petoskey to join other northern Michigan writers and poets on the Red Sky Stage at 445 East Mitchell Street. Inside an old building stands a stage with lighting and sound equipment along with an assortment of hand-me-down chairs and furniture. Around 6:00 pm, people begin to arrive: poets too young to attend without their parents, high school and college creative writing students, laborers, craftsmen, professionals, and retirees. Most of what you will read in this book, I have read on the Red Sky Stage. As both a writer and reader, having an audience means everything—support, feedback, inspiration, and a joyful celebration of creativity in its many forms.

Poems

November, Petoskey, Michigan

The streets have lost their double lining of parked cars.
November turns its cold shoulder, and north wind slams doors.
Dead leaves swarm, gray clouds pile up over the bay, and
 "closed for the season" signs appear in windows of stores.

Sidewalk sales, parades, county fairs, and football season pass.
Cars track new snow in the street. One morning the beach bleaching surf
and the spray over the channel light abruptly stop
at first ice.
The rapids on Bear River narrow, and the town stands in silence.

The News and Review reports the first fisherman to fall through thin ice,
the first hunter to fall out of his tree stand, the first day the ski slopes open.
A child bobs down his first snow hill, falls off at the bottom in delight.
An insurance agent in the attic of an old warehouse addresses calendars.

The young boy at the library on Mitchell Street reads his first lines

of Hemingway, Faulkner, or Fitzgerald, an old man
with dementia stands stationary on the corner, not
knowing where to go next; in a second story loft,
a yoga instructor softly encourages a young woman
dying of cancer.

In a coffee shop, a boy and girl bend their heads
together over hot chocolate;
in the public restroom, a homeless man washes and
changes dirty clothes;
above the general store, an artist stretches his arm to
brushstroke a canvas.
Old friends meet for lunch and hang their coats on
familiar hooks.

In a side street in rehab, men and women confront their
addictions;
on the other end of town, an old woman lays in the
hospice house; nearby
a retired couple walk their dog through the abandoned
streets of Bay View.
Re-sized for winter, we slow our pace, settle in, ease
closer to each other in bed.

Autumn Haiku

Split cordwood scattered
on red leaves and frosted grass
days before winter.

You die in the fall,
your voice greeting still on.
Hear me say I love you.

September clouds
hide the sun then the moon.
Wild creatures know what to do.

Squash soup passing
hints of nutmeg and ginger through my mouth.
Spoon-fed fall.

Autumn on the porch
writing a haiku.
My pen casts a long shadow.

Humming birds gone.
Feeders half full sway in downpour.
Wind chimes play the blues.

Mother turkey in the shade.
One through five survive.
Six, seven, and eight get ate.

Up North Cottage

The deck weathers outside our cottage
where my wife reads the morning paper.
She covers the news with beach rocks, and
wears a sweater against the wind off the lake.

Two hummingbirds hover over the feeder
she has kept so carefully clean all summer.
I watch them suck their sugar juice, each dancing
both separately and together in the autumn air.

"Do they mate in midair?" I ask.
"Watch and tell me," she replies.
The limbs of the beech trees appear awkward
as they reach for the sky and drop their leaves.

Our black lab raises her nose to the air,
and points to the open field (grouse or woodcock I say).
Wood smoke rises from Young State Park
on the far side of the lake. I'd pitch a tent there,

and camp all week, and look across the water to here,
as if this hill were a dream.
But everything is now.
I feel the brisk air stiffen my resolve to do

nothing, owe no one under the white roof of sky,
attend only to deer shadows in the woods,
woods smoke, and windfall from the trees,
no longer waiting and waiting.

Autumn Chill

Leaf falls are stirring, dark clouds
are hurrying, but we
are still.

We have the thoughts of summer,
warmth, and at night
the stars,

and we have limbs, awkward,
funny, reaching
to grow.

But one by one our roots chill,
stiffened by the rain, mine
and yours.

Our sap runs slow. We change
to stone, and numbed
we forget, like cordwood in a fire.

Big trees
are lonely. We have waited years standing
a part.

While we stay rooted, surely
there must be a way we could touch
our boughs,

bend to the lofty light

we share within
our limbs,

touch our bare branches,
taking our chances
before the snow.

October Crossing
Port Clinton to St. Clair Shores

Past yacht masts lighted by flood lamps
with white crosses foreground to a million stars,
the sailboat diesel stutters out the aperture
of the dark harbor on swells from a harvest moon.

Light as wind lift to heron wings,
the mainsail heels us from windward, and splashes
a course to the first marker that bobs in darkness,
secured endlessly and steadfastly to its appointed place.

A red raspberry sunrise mirrors on the water,
then draws its purple redness back to float free
of the horizon, and bounces abaft like a beach ball.
The sky whitens and blues, and the islands green.

Wool warmth gives way to midday sun,
and weather gear stowed, we watch an ore boat
shadow past at a massive pace, a Hong Kong vessel
with a black-capped sailor strolling the decks.

Wind burned, we sway against the blue sky,
float by Detroit Light like a dry leaf,
and enter between two brown fingers of land,
the river that throbs of freighters and foundries.

The distance is nothing. We arrive at the quiet lake,
as the autumn tree line slides away from the sun.

The boat slacks into dockage in the dark as it commenced,
amid yacht masts and stars in symphonic silence.

Greenway, Cotswolds
A Sonnet

November rains are weeping down the hill,
but I want to brave the stormy gusts this day
to find high ground and watch the Severn River fill.
I walk the Stone Age path called Greenway.
My Wellingtons trudge up this time-forgotten hill.
Beyond a cowshed, I look down over the village
shrouded in mist so silvery, silent, and still,
like a painting brushed to life from another Age.
I sit beside a hollowed stump of tree.
Within the stump's circle, a sapling springs
from the grassy space within. Now open and free
from the dark soil below, the new growth sings.
Returning down to where I stay,
I find the fiery hearth in the manor at Greenway.

Still Life

Snow powder shaking from its winter coat,
the deer rises at dawn, haltingly,
snorts steam with frost shimmering
from its flank, white on brown.

Moving from wind shelter of dense thicket,
the deer stamps on thin ice at the lake's edge,
drinks algae-speckled meltwater, then stands
like a statue in the fractured dark of sunrise.

The frozen lake heaves and trembles,
 the rough jagged block field, disjointed and intricate,
cracks the icy surface of polygons and circles,
to echo down-valley the grind of its geometries.

Snow Plows in April

Tree trunks whiskered with wind-whipped snow shiver
half-frozen or half-thawed from the spring storm.

Caught like fish through the ice, the branches quiver
with surprise, awakened as they were in such altered
form.

Between dusk and dawn a foot of new snow fell,
fell on our talk of golf and gardens and spring garb,

clearing the air of new desire, re-freezing what we tell
others we know about life: the old cliché, familiar barb.

Set back by weather, we slow the ascent
to the season of forgetting. The roller coaster stops

at the summit before the arm-raising descent,
and we remember our true selves as God eavesdrops.

Trillium

Erupting angels,

stationary shore birds,

flightless, fanciful, fretless,

regretless egrets.

White, mushrooming,

wind-tossed,

the spring in Spring.

Woman Before a Canvas

One foot forward with brushes in her hands,
she poses before a blank canvas,
waiting in silence before the pulsing white,
the whiteness of white at dawn before color,
the moment between birth and nurture.
She creates but she does not move.
Her eyes are intense as though she surveys
a map of battle, her face steady and strong
as she stands dressed in white, alone
in the presence of God and the world.
Between canvas and artist, the air stirs
like air over ice on a March pond.
Ripe and trembling, alive with new life,
she walks away from the untouched canvas,
herself the work of art.

Detroit Metro
An Ode

Fixed to the floor,
fused forever
to five identical
black and chrome seats,

your frame faces Gate 7
for human lifetimes.
You are sat upon
by manifold people

who foul your surface
with fried food and gum
and chocolate smudges.
But like the earth

you are accustomed
to abuse and refuse and
receive all equally,
thank you very much.

You are the last chair
to support my weary body,
a sure and safe firmament,
before I take flight

into the uncertain air.

Fishing for Wind

The blue-haired woman
with little girl eyes who sat by a walker
with a wide smile, turned to me
speaking over her shoulder
from where she sat on a chair
in the front row like a school girl,
and said she would read poetry
but needed help stepping
up to the stage. She added, smiling,
that she was old, and I replied, smiling,
that I was old, too, but I could help her
up the steps, or she could read from her chair.
She said she wanted the stage.

Once up there, she took command,
adjusted the mic like a pro,
and began to charm everyone
with the strong voice of a woman,
and her words grabbed you hard,
tugged at your heart, made you laugh,
and I could see the high school students
around me respond to the old lady
like fans clapping for a pop star,
and then came her metaphor
that changed the large part of me
that knows no surprises.

The blue-haired lady dropped
a metaphor about children flying kites,

pulling on the strings like fishing for wind,
and the image knocked me off
my quiet easy chair life, and I thought
how I had spent my days fishing for wind,
and how I hated to see a caught bass quiver
and gasp and die, and thought how I had sat
for years in smoke-filled conference rooms
with low ceilings, no windows, and no hope
to go outdoors until the weekend,
and the long business flights looking out
the small plane window on a cold numb sky,
a sky I could not feel, and wind I could not see.

I remembered building a box kite with my dad,
tying the balsam sticks together with string
from my grandfather's butcher shop,
gluing the corners, stretching the plastic
over the frame, painting the plastic
red and silver, smelling the paint and glue,
me spilling the silver paint on the basement floor,
Dad not happy about the floor,
me standing next to the kite,
the kite taller than eight-year-old me,
wondering how an object I could not easily lift
could find wind enough to fly.

And the day all the Indian Guide fathers
drove to the park, and we kids sat on a grassy knoll
falling sideways with laughter as we watched our
fathers running the heavy homemade kites
up and down the field with their leaden feet,

my father huffing, overweight from office work,
my best friend's skinny father running
with a pipe in his mouth, puffing smoke like a
locomotive,
the kites nose diving into the ground digging up turf.

But then, then, a roaring wind snapped,
the gasping, gulping, wind-starved kites,
and they all flew off at once like geese, flying so high
they became black specks in the pale gray sky.
Then our kite broke free of the kite string,
and Dad yelled, "Get in the car!"
so we hopped in the 55 Chevy,
me stretching out the open window looking skyward,
the cold wind blowing against the side of my face,
the lost kite found grounded blocks away,
my eyes filled with tears from the cold wind,
Dad's eyes filled with tears from a small place
somewhere within him.

And the blue-haired woman sat down,
and I wanted to steal her metaphor,
plop it into a poem of my own like a word thief,
but she turned around with her little girl eyes
and wide smile, and I said, smiling, "I like your
metaphor about fishing for the wind," and she said,
smiling, "No metaphor beats the real thing."
Then she reached over her chair,
and handed me a long white package
tied with string, wrapped in butcher paper,
scrawled with instructions that read,

"Open outdoors in a large field with few trees. Add wind and fly."

Short Stories

Big Little Hawk
A Short Story

On a stone-faced bluff in the late Copper Age, a woman lived alone in a hole by a crooked basswood tree. She sat in the cleared field looking out at the bay like a limestone figurine. The level of the lake had been rising for six thousand years before, as the ice sheets from the Ice Age melted, and her hole home was a stone's throw from the beach. Wigwams were for future people, not her. She was one of the last of the Underground People, the ancestors of the Algonquin tribes, remnants disappearing into nothingness like the glacial debris on the beach. Near dark, she rubbed two dry sticks together, and along with the fires of the nearby villagers, the sky turned reddish copper against a sky of low clouds. She lived on the bluff in the late Second Millennium BC, a place where ancient peoples conducted commerce.

The rise where she sat was already old. Formed out of a muddy sea floor in the Middle Devonian Era, the land formed from an accumulation of grayish brown crystalline limestone. Corals were abundant, including *Hexagonaria percarinata*, known by most people as the "Petoskey Stone." The coral forming the stones existed in massive colonies over 350 million years ago, anchored to the bottom in deep-water mud flats, becoming petrified over geologic time. Scoured by glaciers, the stones were left as beach rubble along the shore. The woman traded these as well.

Her name was Big Little Hawk (*Mi-she-pe-pe-quen*), and she lived by trading. She traded seeds, nuts, fish, polished stone axe heads, hammered copper spear points, tools, decorated objects, and human skulls. She protected her hoard with a long, double-edged dagger. People also feared her, because she was said to have dark magical powers. In trade, she received food and beaver skins from hunters, fishermen, and growers of corn and other vegetables. The bravest of the young boys played near her—amusing themselves with footraces, wrestling, and shooting birds, chipmunks, and squirrels with their bows and arrows.

Az taught her trading. He was an Egyptian sailor who came ashore one day alone paddling a bark canoe. When they met, she was bathing at the water's edge. She was fourteen, and unmated. Because of her large size, her mother and father could not find a partner for her. "Az" was the second half of his name. He never told her the first half. He stayed with her until she became pregnant, then paddled away one morning never to be seen again.

Az had been among the Egyptian sailors seeking the pure copper deposited in veins and nuggets of the area's gravel beds, another product of glaciation. The sailors brought copper home to be hammered into axes, points, helmets, shields, breastplates, and to build temples, and statues. Az and his fellow Egyptian sailors were part of a vast trading network including Phoenicians, Trojans, Carthaginians, Greeks,

Babylonians, Cretans, Cypriots, Aegean, Hebrews, Libyans, Arabs, Celts, and Britons who shipped ore and ingots from over 5,000 copper mines in northern Michigan.

Big Little Hawk could not think about thinking, but her limbic brain stem operated in harmony with other parts of her brain and body. She could move her muscles and limbs in perfect balance and coordination, and her hormonal system could release adrenaline in times of stress, fear, excitement, or anger. She could also experience feelings of anger, sadness, joy, and exhilaration, and she could remember these feelings when memory aided her survival. The lobes for her senses were highly developed—smell, taste, touch, sight, and hearing.

Az came from a less primitive civilization in the Mediterranean, and could write the common language of the miners and sailors, reformed Egyptian hieroglyphs (Roots of this ancient language have been found in both the substance and inflections of the Algonquin languages, including both Odawa and Objibwe). Az left behind a copper tablet in this language, buried for the ages in Big Little Hawk's hole in the ground, deep in the bluff overlooking Little Traverse Bay.

Big Little Hawk birthed a baby from Az. One day she went down to the beach to wash clothes. Her little son was strapped to a board, and she sat him down near the water while she worked. The water was very deep next to the shore. As she scrubbed in the water, she turned away from the baby for an instant, and when she turned back, the baby was gone.

She ran up to the basswood tree and shouted for help. The Underground People looked far and wide, but the baby could not be found. The same day the baby was lost, an earthquake rocked the land. People in the village said they could hear a baby crying under the ground. They said it was Big Little Hawk's baby. The magicians of the village met around a fire where they lit their pipes and rattled tambourines. They called upon spirits, and the spirits told them that Big Little Hawk had hidden her baby in the ground and made the earth tremble. From then on, the villagers feared her as a monstrous baby killer with magical powers. They also feared going near what the villagers called "the hole."

One day, Big Little Hawk plunged into Little Traverse Bay and disappeared. She entered the water to look for life. She grasped at the rocks on the lake bottom to hold herself down while looking for her son. For days afterwards, her wolf-bred dog searched for her with its nose close to the ground, running back and forth on the beach. Big Little Hawk could not liberate herself from the deep loss of her baby son. Only the copper tablet of Az remained, buried for thousands of years, now lying beneath a construction site in downtown Petoskey, Michigan.

Mikage's Escape
A Short Story

Mikage walked along the waterfront and out to the end of the long pier every day. The oceanfront in Santa Cruz, California smelled like the shore or the wharf or the town depending on the weather, and sometimes the time of day. During the cool wet winters, the momentous surf pounded the beach bringing along the smell of salt mixed with water, sea creatures and briny kelp. In summer with an overcast, foggy sky, the cooking smells from the sea markets ruled the mornings and afternoons along with wood smoke from the state park. And at other times, when the days were long and nights short, an offshore evening breeze freshened the honeysuckle-scented bougainvillea and mixed with pine scents from mountain forests by the sea. On those days, the clouds of crinkled pinkish-lavender flowers reminded Mikage of the stories her parents told her about Japan:

"I liked living in Japan. When I was your age, we lived next to a park," her father once said.

Mikage's mother added, "We were still young in our marriage, and every morning we would get up at five and take a walk. On the weekends, we would pack a lunch of cucumber salad and soupy rice, and have a picnic surrounded by flowers and cherry trees."

"Yes, we drank tea and chatted for hours until we felt sluggish, then napped on our tatami mats under the sky," said Mikage's father.

"And sometimes we would sing a little song about drifting in a boat in the moonlight," said Mikage's mother. Mikage pictured how her mother's eyes had beamed with remembrance.

"And one day we stayed until night, and were surprised by the streaks of a shooting star," her father said, "then we kissed and kissed and kissed." Mikage smiled when she thought how embarrassed she had been when her father talked about kissing.

Mikage loved to watch people relaxing either alone or together on the beach—fishing, kayaking, surfing, bicycling, drinking wine or beer while eating seafood in the restaurants, or sunning on the beach, playing Frisbee, or beach volleyball. She loved to watch the seals, sea lions, and otters with their bottomless black eyes and fleshy snouts around and below the boardwalk. In the background, you could hear the wind-muffled screams of children as they rode the rides at the amusement park, the more distant jingling sound of rigging on sailboat masts rocking in the marina, and the sputtering of fishing boats motoring out for rock bass on the kelp beds.

Mikage loved to bring tea in a thermos, and buy a fried artichoke heart to munch while sitting on the seawall. The beach always cheered her up; the pastel buildings around the carousel and roller coaster, the white rolling surf, the stucco houses along the street, Tibetan prayer flags blowing in one of the backyards, the large red "Boardwalk" sign that curved over the foot of Beach Street, the beach dotted with sandpipers running down to the turquoise Pacific. This was one of her favorite places anywhere. It shimmered of a life lived best.

Axel met Mikage on the beach in Santa Cruz in August 1966. Axel was in his mid-thirties; Mikage only twenty-four. He noticed the lithe young girl with crescent eyes, and shiny black hair watching him, as he strutted, jumped and dove playing volleyball. He left the others and approached her, his tan, lean body dusted with sand. He appeared god-like with his blond hair sifting the bright sun as he walked. He shuffled over to her, and asked her all the usual questions in a formal, courteous way, his light blue eyes unblinking. His German accent was crisp, but he sometimes scrambled English syntax and pronounced certain words in foreign ways. Since Mikage was proficient in languages, she had heard his Southern German accent. He had a nice, self-deprecating sense of humor, and laughed often as he talked. He suggested that they should meet somewhere, and so on the following Friday evening and she suggested her parents' sushi restaurant in Capitola. She had been raised to be wary of strangers, so the restaurant would be safe.

Mikage's parents had been interned in 1942 to a "War Relocations Camp" following Japan's attack on Pearl Harbor. Her mother was pregnant with Mikage who was born later that year. Because of their Japanese ancestry, the US Government removed them from their home and restaurant business in San Francisco, even though they were American citizens. Mikage was barely a toddler when she and her parents arrived at the Heart Mountain Relocation Center in the northwest corner of Wyoming in 1944. She, along with over 10,000 other Japanese Americans, half of which were children, lived in this internment camp sixty miles east of Yellowstone Park until the center closed in 1945. Her parents then returned to the Bay Area, and started their business again.

During their first dinner, Axel told his story almost like an outline he had rehearsed: how his father, an SS Officer, had disappeared after World War II, how his mother had raised him in a small village in Southern Germany on the Lake of Constance that he called *Bodensee*, how he was an only child, and one of a few children in the area. A good student, he graduated from the University of Konstanz with a degree in economics. After working two years for a small automotive electronics company near Radolfzell, he applied for and later graduated from the MBA Program at Stanford University. After a brief stint with a large international consulting firm, he returned to Germany, and progressed with unusual speed to managing director at an optical firm based in Konstanz. He had returned to the Bay Area for his first long vacation.

At Axel's bidding, Mikage described her childhood after the internment camp, growing up near the Mission District in San Francisco, and along with her two younger brothers, helping out with the family business. When she was a teenager, her parents had moved out to Capitola, and opened a new restaurant there only a few blocks from the ocean.

Her modesty did not permit her to convey her special linguistic gifts. By her sophomore year in college, Mikage had mastered French, Italian, German, Dutch, Russian, Persian, Swahili, Indonesian, Hindi, Ojibwa, Pashto, and Turkish in addition to the English and the Japanese her family spoke. Her professors at San Jose State told her she belonged to a small "neural tribe" of people throughout the world with brains wired to master multiple languages with ease, a step beyond multilingual. Language experts called these gifted people "hyper polyglots" She taught high school French and German at the high school in Santa Cruz.

Axel asked, "How did you get to be so tall?"

"My parents fed me well. They were in charge of the relocation camp gardens. They surrounded the barren camp barracks with beautiful and bountiful gardens that included stones, flowers, and a pool of water. They also planted some small fruit trees, willow trees, and shrubs, and I was small enough for them to shelter me from the sun. The gardens were fertilized with egg shells and tea leaves, and protected from the rabbits by wire, scavenged and turned into homemade fences. The gardens kept us from sinking into dust. I ate raw vegetables every day—carrots, broccoli, green beans, lettuce, tomatoes, cantaloupe, strawberries and raspberries."

"Your parents must have been strong people."

"Strong and good. My father often said to me, 'Small treasures correct great tragedies.' I was their treasure."

She was attracted to Axel, but she knew from the beginning he was a bit strange. He showed up at the restaurant with a typed agenda detailing what he wanted to cover. Mikage liked to be organized, but this was a bit too much like a business meeting. At the end of the evening, they shook hands, and she told him she would like to see him again, but added, "Oh, Axel, please, no more agendas!" Her parents were impressed with Axel, because of his formality and manners, but Mikage still remained unsure for a long time. There was something about him that gave her a feeling of sand getting sucked into the backwash of a wave.

For the next three years, Mikage and Axel dated, taking turns flying back and forth between the States and Germany. Axel professed his love to her often, and asked her to marry him more than once. Mikage would reply, "Not before winter. Maybe spring or summer." Then Axel gave her an ultimatum—either she married him, or he would move on. Mikage raised her small hands to settle on top of his, and she finally said yes.

Axel's mother flew to California for the wedding, and after a two-day honeymoon in Vancouver, Mikage moved with Axel to Germany where they found a small apartment across from a church in the center of Konstanz. The apartment had high ceilings, large windows, beautiful marble floors, and since Axel was doing well financially, they bought high quality contemporary furnishings. Mikage brought energy and cheerfulness to setting up a household in this part of the world that was so new to her.

Axel, however, treated their marriage as a project on a critical path chart. Now that he possessed the respectability of marriage, he placed greater priority on his career, and the select co-workers and friends who could support his aspirations. He turned off his charm like a rocker switch on his Mercedes, his eyes focused on the fast and wide autobahn of ambition. No speed limits, no curves—straight lines. She was on the third tier of his mind's organization chart of who was important. Axel disappointed her: both the little girl in her who wanted romance and marriage, and the grown woman part of her who wanted to be deeply loved and respected.

One evening many years later, Mikage lit a soy candle, and wrote about the events leading to their break-up in her diary:

—*From Mikage Hoshimoto's diary, 1 May 2007—*

Axel used to call me *"Sweetie Pie."* He hurt me so much calling me this. When we had our weekly Saturday morning scheduled sex, he called me this. I now remember Axel hovering over me, then tilling inside me. I knew he cheated on me. I could detect which lover he had been with during the week by his movements—the slow, deep thrusts were thanks to Doris, the shallow, fast ones, Renate's. I felt like I was dirty, making love with the bodies of other women mixed up with him. During these thoughts, he would announce his impending orgasm: *Sweetie Pie, I will be coming soon,* as if he was making a weather forecast.

One morning, as I lay flat on my back fulfilling what Axel called his 'marital obligation,' I could see my sweet parakeet, Gino, circling near the ceiling as he prepared his weekly dive bomb attack on Axel. Gino was jealous of this weekend intruder on our peaceful, quiet life together. Gino landed on Axel's back, swooping down in perfect timing before the big event, pecking at Axel, scolding him, fluttering his little wings. *"Mein Got, I will twist his goddam head off!"* Axel yelled as he put his fists together and wrenched them in opposite directions. It was all too much at once.

I started yelling back at him. Gino was shaking. I was shaking. I told Axel that I hated him for keeping me caged like a bird, for living in this little town where the shops were open only a few hours a day, where the church bells chimed every fifteen minutes. I told him I dreaded the silence, waiting for the chimes to ring again. I told him I felt tormented, compelled to sound out on schedule like the church bells, to do his laundry, iron his shirts, clean the house, fix his meals, give him sex, and go to business dinners where my presence was needed to translate for visitors. "What do you think of my pretty little executive wife?" Axel would say.

I felt like a mechanical bell no one listened to, but still compelled to ring four times each hour. I told him that I feared someday I would become so dull that I would not even ring as the bells rang across our street. After fifteen years of marriage, he still had no idea what I was talking about. He said he liked the bell tower. With his superiority complex and my inferiority complex, we were locked in as tight as our German plumbing fixtures.

One night we were driving across the Swiss border for dinner. Axel kept asking, "Sweetie Pie, did you remember your passport?"

Yes, Axel, I have my passport, I kept telling him and would pull it out of my purse to show him.

When we arrived at the border crossing, he turned white, and said, "*Mein Got,* I have forgotten my passport!" Axel tried to persuade the border guard to let us through, but his superior tone of voice worked against him. We had to turn around and go home. "Why didn't you remind me?" he asked angrily.

Each year our time together as man and wife became more silent and much more difficult. At one point, I talked with Axel about having a baby, but he said babies were unsanitary. I started taking long walks, brooding along the edges of the town, trying to be a good wife with occasional lapses of bitterness, all compounded by not having anything meaningful to do and no friends, a pitiful, calamitous, and incurable situation.

—From Mikage Hoshimoto's diary, 2 April 2007—

Our marriage ended on a festive day. A few weeks after I told Axel off, it was May on the *Bodensee*, and the poplars were blooming and swaying tall over the lake. You could see Switzerland from the German side of the lake, and the bells ringing from there in the distance moved over the water light and soft, with a resonance that disappeared into a dreamy silence. These sights and sounds gave me moments of respite from the sad life I had been living. I was still very unhappy, and while the day-to-day suffering had become familiar, and deep within, I found a little tune that I could play each day that was mine, and only mine. I felt like there was a part of me that was solid and still, shiny like a bell, given to me by the resilience of both Mom and Dad. Even though I knew Axel would resist, I had a private dream to open a small wine pub in the village, where I could serve traditional Japanese food that my parents had taught me to prepare. The kitchen smells from the nearby Gasthaus triggered my memories.

During this first week in May, when the tourists started to reappear, I suggested to Axel that we go sailing in the little red sail boat we kept near the center of Konstanz. I could see the German boats crossing to the Swiss side for picnics, and the Swiss boats coming ashore along the German side. It was a sunny, festive day, and we pushed off in the direction of Mainau, "*the flower island.*" The lake was filled with meltwater from the snow-capped Alps, which were visible as a backdrop to the gray, icy water that was lapping against the peeling paint of our boat. As we slacked into shore, thousands of flowers bloomed everywhere—pansies, daisies, forget-me-nots, wallflowers, tulips, rhododendrons, and peonies, all patterned in beds that were tended with care. I remember seeing an orange-throated hummingbird. The island reminded me of the park my parents had described in Japan, the one where they relaxed and enjoyed being with each other. Loving each other and laughing together.

People were visiting the Orchid Show in the Palm House. Naked little boys and girls played with toy boats, and shrieked when their hands or feet touched the cold waters. Older people were walking along the footpaths: women in their flowered dresses and kerchiefs, men with their old-fashioned cloth caps and walking sticks, and a few wearing lederhosen. Everyone seemed to be walking in one direction, circling the island from right to left. Axel and I spread a blanket out on the luscious lawn, and I took out a basket from the boat filled with California rolls that I prepared, a bottle of Riesling, a bottle of Himbeergeist, a German liquor that was made with strong spirits and raspberries, and my thermos of tea. I placed the bottles in the cold lake water nearby. Axel removed his shirt. His once sculpted torso that I had first seen on the beach in Santa Cruz looked like the sagging skin of a boiled chicken.

Later, I had asked Axel if he would like any more California rolls, since he had consumed a half bottle of the wine on a nearly empty stomach.

"Yes, Mikage, but more wine also—this hot sun is making me thirsty." He finished the bottle while criticizing my preference for green tea. He kept on, "You should have brought beer. This is a day for *beer,* not wine; but, of course, my pretty American wife is *too refined* for beer. Beer is for Germans, right, ha, ha, ha. We are not so good as you, *Sweetie Pie.* You are *immer besser.*"

As the morning slowly turned into afternoon, Axel began to express disapproval of everything and everyone around him by judging the flowers, the gardeners, the men, women, and children who passed by: foreign flowers, foreign people, swollen bellies, skinny legs. "The guest workers are all parasites," he said loudly. When he tired of this, he asked for the schnapps, and drank it out of his wine glass rather than the my tiny, decorative sipping glasses that I had bought at Meersburg. Axel was always nasty and difficult, but he was worse when drunk.

Like men his age, he often said that a "home was a man's castle," but he was never content when he was home.

—*From Mikage Hoshimoto's diary, 5 May 2007*—

We returned to the apartment amid churchgoers from the cathedral. We all strolled towards our homes. The sound of the church bells jarred me. Sunday afternoon was the only unplanned part of our week, and Axel began fidgeting, as if the rest of the day was a barren desert that he had to cross on foot. He scurried around the apartment like a hyperactive hamster spinning on a wheel. Then Axel stopped. He looked up at the top of our curtain rod, and said, "That damned bird!" Gino was perched above him, his little bird heart thumping, his eyes fixed on Axel. "Mikage, why don't you keep that bird caged?"

"He *is* in a cage," I replied. "The cage is this apartment, and he's free to roam around it, and breathe and eat and sleep like we do." I couldn't believe I was saying this. Maybe aversion for keeping Gino locked up came from my experience as a little girl trapped behind barbed wire and guard towers, or feeling trapped in a marriage lacking love or affection. Axel wanted everything and everyone in our tiny apartment in its proper place. When I moved from one room to the next, I felt like a trespasser in my own home.

Axel began to swat at Gino with my tennis racquet. I asked Axel to stop. Gino thrashed and darted up and down in the high-ceilinged sitting room looking for safety. Gino made matters worse by defecating on Axel's head, but he had to be nervous.

"I will kill the Arschgeige!" Axel screamed. I vomited, an event he ignored.

As a little girl in the internment camp, I would sit by a brush fire outdoors to get away from our tarpaper row house. Every once in a while, the firewood would shift and fall into the center of the pit. There would be smoke at first, and then a flame would burst and emit intense heat. This is how I felt at that moment. I knew with clarity that our marriage had caved, and that I had to protect Gino, my only comfort in Germany.

I knew what I had to do. Axel kept a loaded Lugar pistol in a wooden box in our dresser. I walked into the bedroom, removed the gun, and returned as Axel batted Gino to the floor. He was about to stomp on Gino, when I fired the gun into our walnut display case of colored wine goblets.

As the bells across the street began to toll, the shards of glass formed a bright-colored mosaic on the white marble floor. Axel's pink face turned zombie white with rage. His eyes were bloodshot from drinking. Without thinking, I fired the gun a second time into the center of his framed Stanford diploma, and a third time into the Black Forest cuckoo clock with the obnoxious little painted bird that kept popping out to frighten Gino each hour. The whole apartment filled with a blue haze of gun smoke. I said to Axel, "You should have guessed by now the reason I know so many languages. I am a trained assassin, and I will demonstrate my skills to you."

"*Gottverdammt!*"

Axel fainted in a heap on the floor. Gino flew out an open window. I checked into the guest house down the street, and for three days, I circled the neighborhood until I found Gino. We flew to California. Gino died a two years later. Axel and I had been married for fifteen years, but the divorce was simple, because I had wanted nothing but my freedom. I resumed my teaching position at the high school in Santa Cruz, then followed a love interest to Michigan after my parents died. He was a kind but dull man. I dumped him within a year. I started a diner in a small mill town, and found friends who appreciated me. I have a little genius within me who likes to cook. So, this is my life story up until now.

One-Act Play

Wanting to Be Liked
A One-Act Play

CHARACTERS:
Alan Matthews
Stanley Sly
Louise, Stanley's Secretary
Edgar, Alan's father (not seen)

SCENE: A dim office with high ceilings and factory windows bordered by sun-faded floor-to-ceiling draperies. Oriental rugs cover the floor and built-in bookcases line the walls. A large oak desk centered in the office in front of a dark green leather-upholstered, high back office chair. Two brown leather upholstered high-back chairs sit on the other side of the desk. The desk is back dropped with high bookcases filled with black binders and hardbound books with frayed covers and broken spines. A side chair sits to the left of the desk. A secretarial desk sits back right, and perpendicular to the desk there is a stand with an old-style mechanical typewriter sitting on top. Beyond the desk further back left is a modest junior manager's desk and armless desk chair with a telephone on top. The offices are located on the second-floor corner of an office headquarters attached to the largest factory of a Midwest military contractor. The office space and desks are free of clutter. It is early afternoon on a rainy day in 1979. [Note: the office looks like a museum of an office from the 1930s.]

At the rise of the curtain, Alan stands near one of the bookcases inspecting the book titles. Louise taps the typewriter keys at her desk, and hits the carriage return after each line of type. She is wearing a gray suit with shoulder pads and high-heeled shoes. She is a short, trim woman in her seventies. Alan stands tall and thin, dressed in a Navy blue suit and rep tie, his black wing-tipped shoes shine like a mirror.

LOUISE *(formally)*: Mr. Sly is on his way back from a meeting at The University Club downtown. He hates meetings, and he hates downtown. He'll be here soon. He always gets up and leaves meetings if they run over. I would offer you coffee, but Mr. Sly doesn't like people who drink coffee.

ALAN: I don't drink coffee. I don't mind waiting.

LOUISE: You don't smoke, do you? He doesn't like people who smoke either. I used to smoke, but I had to quit. He said anyone who has time to smoke can't possibly be a good worker. Do you drink coffee?

ALAN: I don't . . .

LOUISE: Yes, you said that before, didn't you?

ALAN *(respectfully)*: No, I don't smoke. I need time to organize my notes. Look at all these books!

LOUISE: Good books, aren't they? I decorated the office, except for the books. The books are Mr. Sly's.

ALAN: Yes, classics, and I like the decorations, the sporting prints especially.

LOUISE: Actually, all the paintings are originals.

ALAN: I don't understand much about art. I ought to know more. Right now, I'm trying to learn about business.

LOUISE *(wryly)*: Mr. Sly started this business as a bicycle shop. Then he started making parts for cars and airplanes. He's very smart, and has opinions on everything. You should know, he doesn't like two-way conversations. Be prepared to listen, young man, and do what he tells you to do. Mr. Sly criticizes his managers for talking when they should be listening. He listens to me when I make him listen, but my concerns aren't that important. Of course, I would like an increase in pay for how hard I work. He's not easy to work for, you know. I know why you're here today.

After Louise leaves Sly's inner office, Alan takes an economics book off the shelf, and starts reading, then drops the book when Stanley Sly bursts through a side door to the right, and walks briskly towards his chair, no handshake and no eye contact. He is 94 years old with combed-back white hair, and wears large black-framed glasses over floppy ears. He wears a blue gray three-piece suit with a colorful tie and powder blue shirt. He has an athletic gait to his walk, but his face looks older than death. He is about five foot six. Sitting down behind the desk, he folds his long arthritic fingers in his lap, and opens his mouth to speak. His eyes appear out of focus. Alan replaces the book, and follows Stanley's eye motions instructing him to sit down in the side chair next to his desk.

STANLEY: *I'm late! I hate people who are late, don't you? I was downtown at a meeting, and I hate meetings and I hate downtown, don't you?*

ALAN: I don't know.

STANLEY: You're not supposed to answer a rhetorical question. What are we about today, young man? That's a question you can answer.

ALAN *(enthusiastically)*: I'm the new Personnel Director, and we need to review your secretary's salary for next year.

Stanley reaches into his desk drawer, and pulls out a clean sheet of white paper. He hands it to Alan.

STANLEY *(looking impatient)*: Very well, you write down the information, and then I'll comment on it.

Alan writes Louise's salary history and the guidelines for the next year on the piece of paper.

ALAN *(earnestly)*: Well sir, this shows Louise's salary history for the last three years, and the guidelines for next year.

STANLEY: *She makes that much?* I tell you Democrats are ruining this country. Now I hate coat hangers. You reach into the closet for one, and three fall on the floor—but coat hangers are more intelligent than a Democrat. Now Louise isn't very bright, but at my age, I don't need a bright secretary *(the background typing stops)*. I give her dictation twice a day. Since I'm hard of hearing and she's blind as a bat, she types something that is unintelligible. Now you may ask...why do I still come to the office every day and send out memos? Because if our profits go down, I'll have to go back to work. *(Typing resumes, more banging than tapping.)*

ALAN *(cautiously)*: So, are you planning to make an adjustment—in her salary?

STANLEY: I suppose so...but not this year...maybe next. Besides, Louise forgets to open the drapes in the morning, and close them before she goes home. I can't support this kind of negligence. By the way, have you noticed that all the windows in this office building have been replaced except for these original factory windows in my office? Why do you suppose that is? Tell me—*do you think I can't afford new windows?*

ALAN: I don't know, Mr. Sly, why? I'm sure you can buy new windows if you want to.

STANLEY *(loudly with feeling)*: The windows are a *symbol of the way things used to be!* I hate all the expense of showing off. I hate marketing. I hate lawyers and accountants. I hate unions. I hate all this talk of corporate responsibility. When I formed this company, we had one goal: to make a profit. Now we have to hire women, minorities and other feeble-minded people. To me the greatest sight in the world would be to see all the dark-skinned people in this country swimming past the Statue of Liberty back to where they came from with a liberal under each arm. And as for women, why before World War II, all the secretaries were men, and they were damn good secretaries. Women have no place outside the home. (*He leans forward in a confidential tone of voice.*) Do you know that last Friday night, I walked into Kelly's office to find the old boy on top of his secretary on top his desk? That's what happens when you mix men and women at work. Now we have to do the right thing. *Fire Kelly's secretary!*

ALAN *(stunned)*: Mr. Sly, that's not right.

STANLEY *(patronizingly)*: Well then, give her two weeks' pay.

ALAN *(grim)*: We need to be even-handed on this. Things are different these days.

STANLEY *(gruffly)*: You talk too much. Now let me tell you a thing or two about what we're doing around here. You'll learn more if and when you pass your security clearance. We're making drives for torpedoes in this factory. We ship them to another factory in Minneapolis where they get loaded with warheads. This new torpedo blows out the water thirty feet under the hull of an enemy ship. The ship collapses into the vacuum. Pretty nifty, eh? The idea came from the sinking of that freighter in Lake Superior several years ago—the Edmund Fitzgerald collapsed in troughs between high waves. So now we can blow big holes under enemy ships. Important work, wouldn't you say? Now I'll tell you what I think about you—under your navy blue suit and silk tie lurks a hippie. I bet you did drugs and sex in college, protested for civil rights and against Vietnam. Tell me I'm right.

ALAN: Mr. Sly, I didn't like Vietnam much after I got shot down in a helicopter twice. Two tours were enough for me. I did drugs like most of the others, but there wasn't much opportunity for sex in the jungle.

STANLEY: What were you doing in Vietnam in helicopters? Couldn't your father get you out of the draft?

ALAN: No, I guess he didn't know anyone important like you. Someone always has to do the dirty work. Our unit crossed into Cambodia to chase deserters, and when we found them, we killed them. That's right. We killed them. So your business is child's play in comparison. *(typing stops)*

STANLEY: I didn't catch everything you said, but I didn't like your tone. You said something about child's play, didn't you? Now, I'm going to change the subject to let you off the hook. I happen to like mental exercises. Try this one...does your office have a window?

ALAN: No sir.

STANLEY: *Well, pretend you have one!* Now imagine you've been fired. It's a snowy winter day, and you're looking through your office window from the outside. You're feeling cold and standing in the dark, and you're watching the man who replaced you doing all the things you had failed to do. Now...go back to your office and do all those things before you get *fired!* *(typing resumes)*. And one more thing—I heard people around here seem to like you—do you want to be liked?

ALAN: Yes.

STANLEY: *Exactly* what I suspected. When you want to be liked, you have a personality defect—*pure vanity!* Personal kindness cannot be tolerated in a tough-minded executive. Softness is like an infectious disease. Sooner or later, you'll start making decisions based on concerns for people rather than concerns for results. And at the end of the day, you'll end up hurting the people you want to help. Once I succumbed to that failing. I liked all the boys in the marketing department, even though they were incompetent fools. Then one day, because of their stupid mistakes, I had to lay off an entire shift in the factory. No, you have to be tough in business. No place for bleeding hearts. If you want to get somewhere, stop wanting to be liked or go into social work where you can be a softy!

Alan makes an about face, and exits the office. Once outside, he passes Louise without eye contact, and walks back to his desk. She follows him with her eyes, wondering about her raise. He calls Edgar, his father. In the meantime, Stanley jumps out of his chair, and exits right briskly, mumbling in an irritated tone about having to attend another meeting.

EDGAR: Hello?

ALAN *(somberly)*: Dad, I don't like my new job. I'm going to quit.

EDGAR: Alan...you'll be throwing your career away. You don't want a reputation as a job hopper. And don't forget about your wife and children and student loans. Sometimes, you need to let things drop to get along.

ALAN: Dad, you didn't raise me the way you did to work in a place like this.

EDGAR: Son, we all have complaints about work—it's kind of like a rocky marriage. Everything's not pretty at the telephone company either, but I've worked here for forty years. You can't go to work every day and open yourself up to a moral crisis. Don't take things so seriously.

ALAN *(puzzled)*: Why? I don't understand.

EDGAR: You trade your loyalty for a steady job so you can buy a house and a car, take care of your family, and pay your bills. You keep your mouth shut. You learn to be tough.

ALAN: So that's how you play the game?

EDGAR *(reflectively)*: Yes, we play the game, all of us. When I served on a tin can destroyer in the Pacific, I didn't agree with all of what we did. Near the end of the war, we accidentally shelled a POW camp on the Japanese coast filled with Americans. Big mistake. Killed thirty of our own people. But we survived the war by doing what we were told, even if the officers didn't know shit from Shinola. You have to follow orders and keep flexible. The man you work for has been on the cover of news magazines. I wish I had worked with someone like him when I was younger.

ALAN: I've followed your advice about most things, Dad ...but I don't like the people here.

EDGAR: Think it over for a few days. It takes forty years to build a good pension and retiree benefits. And people notice when you leave a company with a good reputation. They think you did something wrong. Your career will be under a cloud. Now then, I hope you don't leave, but if you do, I could try to get you in here at the phone company. There's nothing much you can object to about a public utility. It's almost like working for a bank.

ALAN: I didn't do anything wrong. I don't want to be under a cloud. I do want to be liked. How can that be wrong?

EDGAR: I know you'll do the right thing *(he hangs up)*.

ALAN: I want to wake up every day and like myself and the world. Life must have more potential than getting a job with benefits, and living the same life as my dad. I'm terribly sorry I went to work here. I had no idea. Everyone seemed so nice when I interviewed. I guess you can be anybody under a nice suit.

Alan hangs up the phone. He lays his head over his folded arms. The office has gone quiet. After a few beats, he rises abruptly and exits stage right.

THE END

Fable

Trella

Love Fable of an Oak Tree

People stump by on frozen leaves and snow. I see a man drag a fresh-cut pine from the forest. The half-dead tree screams murder. I hear the tree scream, because I am a tree. Two red-cheeked children, a boy and girl, follow after the man and a woman. The man and woman walk apart in silence. The children jangle words. The man and woman look dark, thin as shadows. The round children follow, hopping like large white rabbits. The man carries a saw shaped like a harp, but he's no angel.

The man turns his head around and snarls at the little girl. The little girl cries. She dries tears thick as sap with her fists. The man and woman pass. The children pass. Their heads bob up and down below me, and then they fall away and drop into shadows. The cut off pine tree had been within my view, and so my world changes. I groan to see my friend the pine tree gone.

When a tree around me falls and dies, light plays in different ways on my limbs and trunk, and I can see the beyond of what had been hidden from me. Behind the frayed skinny stump of the absent tree, I see more trees, large and small, light-starved saplings, brown rotting windfalls, green mossy rocks, a silvery spider web, and black bugs creeping around in the dazzle of unfamiliar, golden light.

I hear the faint, wind-swallowing voices of the children behind me, and the sounds of shutting doors. *Slam, slam, slam*, and a *SLAM*. I hear the start of a machine engine, and the sound of wheels cracking ice, a brief rush of noise in an age of normal silence. I think the man and woman may have loved each other once, but not now. I know this, because I am a large tree, and I have a mind full of thoughts, and a trunk full of feelings. I know something about love, and in my mid-most middle, the problem love causes trees.

I do not pretend to solve the trouble with trees, but only to present the problem from the sparse view of what surrounds me—nothing too wild or too grand. No big answers to large questions. All I know is without knowledge. I piece life together one moment at a time in the light and dark, and in the light in between: the first light of day break and the last light of evening and the amber light of middle day. I remain planted on a small rise of ground mid great and small rhythms of life around and below me. And above me, I see the sun, moon, and all things in the unbounded sky. I live simply, rooted deep down in the world of earth.

Nothing I have to say is more than the sense of a knobbed old tree. Summer sun tans my crusty bark to a brownish gray. Autumn rains chill my roots. The hoary frost and snow of winter cover my bark. My awkward limbs and roots reach to grow in the warmth of spring, and the splashing rain soaks me. I see beauty around me, but a limited and personal beauty, because the whole of me is one tree in one place. I have modest dreams, limited experiences, no high dramas, and no adventures. I fear little and hope less.

Some days, I am grateful for boredom. The boring days have neither noise nor silence, but the equal music of nature, and there is an equal light that neither glares nor darkens. On these days, I might expect things to stay much the same forever in one vertical eternity, no beginning or ending but one ever-turning earth. One upright tree in the forest, an untraveled finite particle of infinite nature. I also know that one day, I will fall out of time—a tree fallen in the forest to become planks for the floor of a house or slats for a swing or some stiff-backed object that requires real wood like a chest of drawers. Who knows what happens to one tree?

A word about my life. My coarse furrowed and ridged trunk stands straight at the bottom, but a bit stooped beneath the weight of my crown, which resembles an immense unfurled umbrella, freckled by sunlight, held up against the unrelenting pull of gravity. Spring and summer leaves cloak my canopy so you cannot see the pattern of my branches, twigs, and finer twig-lets. I broke through the ruined world of the forest floor 180 years ago, beginning life like an ordinary woody vegetable or some ridiculous species of weed. I was a scrawny miracle, not because I was a one-of-a-kind birth, but because I survived when many died.

With full growth, the mass of swaying upper limbs on my stocky shoulders can be a weighty, complicated burden when the wind blows hard, swooping me up towards the sky at rakish angles. Upholding is not for the faint.

My likes and dislikes: I like wet and warm, rather than cold and dry. In dry times I absorb the life out of what lives around me. In wet times, I provide shelter for jays, and acorns for foraging squirrels. I am an oak tree—warped and jagged, but still a fine tower of a tree. I shade a large area with the power to steal the sun, to bloom or wither those under my leafy treedom. But more than the whole of all, I have learned to love.

Trella grew nearby. When she was a tiny sapling, she was not easy to care about or love. It's easy to love a deer, or a tall mountain, or a clear lake surrounded by pinewoods, but loving something awkward and small like bugs or moles or a fern or a puddle of muddy water, or ugly things in general, is more difficult...or getting close to something that could die the next day, that could die in the dark, or break in the morning frost. So I didn't think much about Trella for years. She was like a long-legged girl who seemed to grow an inch an hour. I would call her youthful appearance more branchy than beautiful, like an awkward girl not grown up.

In a few decades, Trella waxed into a lithe and lively cottonwood tree. Unlike a slow-growing oak tree like me, she grew fast, 60 feet to my 80. While I grew wide, she grew *wonderly* high. Her leaves shaped into diamonds that slivered the sunlight around us, and crumbled up the moon's face into a thousand white stars. For fifty years, she stood by my side, and my love for her grew as trees grow, by a little bit each season, because for trees, love like truth grows slow. But one spring when birds gathered in her branches, and her limbs thickened with leaves, I discovered her in a new way. And when the wind bent our heads together, I felt strangely warmed inward to my mid-most pith, shook with permanent gladness to be near her, and to be caressed by her soft billowing blossoms. She was so lovely, so lively...so living.

My leaves trembled with awestruck joy. Her buoyant canopy of emerald leaves felt soft and feathery. Her silhouette of braided leaves and limbs enfolded and tickled leathery me. She drove me half-crazy from her teasing brushes, and when she egged me to close my eyes, and blew her fluffy seeds in my face, I came as close to rapture as a tree can get. You need to wonder what she saw in me—besides my location. I felt vague and unsure beside her, but I knew that she loved me, because of the way she kept brushing her willowy branches against me. Sometimes we would get lost in each other, hardwood and softwood, entangled in love; my friend and lover, my brother and sister.

But nothing lasts forever. The trouble days come.

On an overcast day in late autumn, when the rain could not be said to stop or start, heavy-footed *forsters* lumbered into the dull light with eyes like cold gray stones. The thick-chested men carried spinning chain engines on their arms, and a smell not of nature they carried with them. I was not astonished. I had seen them before. They were looking to slay pulpwood. They appeared out of place in the forest, not of our world. They oozed out of their tight clothes. In the damp sky, Trella and I stood like bare naked lovers with our long limbs exposed, except for the few leaves that still tugged on barren us for dear life.

The frozen-hearted *forsters* ripped Trella apart. Her upper limbs fell like leaves. The ground shook when her slaughtered trunk toppled, then slammed into the brushwood. They made a wreck of her. She was all over the place. I felt like I might split down my middle. I could almost hear her heart center stop beating as she sprawled sun-faced down, covered by straddles of her own branches, her light-hungry leaves dying in the shadows. The *forsters* stood around laughing like devils in a field of hell.

I was so angry, I wanted to straighten my trunk and drop a limb on them. I wanted to do some fierce and revengeful thing to them, terrible and swift...but I'm no more than a looker, watching the whole show staged by what's beyond my line of sight. It was a grim trouble-day when Trella died. Rather than dying from harsh nature, she died on a logger's whim. She died *cwik* as a rainbow. I have no more but her.

This quiet morning, a crescent day moon sits above me. The day moon glows like a round moon with a piece missing; a broken moon. Ashes of clouds wisp across the moon face with the missing piece. From experience, I know that the moon will grow round again, and in the spring, I know that out of Trella's woody ruins, sapling branches will sprout from her roots to form their own shadows. The saplings will grow cottony seeds, and the cottony seeds will grow small buds, and the small buds will swell and thicken and grow shoots. I will see Trella again in the close comfort of new growth. I will learn to love small and ugly things again. I will remember a half-forgotten feeling— that I was once loved completely. The soft face of nature will keep me.

I know that summer will arrive again. I will take what comes, because I have no choice. That is the problem of trees.

Memoir (excerpt)

Out of the Inferno: A Husband's Passage Through Cancerland

(an excerpt from Red Sky Series, Book 2)

1.

Stopped mid-motion in the middle
Of what we call our life…

Dante's Inferno, Canto I

On a rainy November day in central Texas, Neil Schmitt, my father-in-law, trudged wearily down a country road along Pecan Bayou. A tall, lean man, he bent his head against the rain. He wore a floppy hunting cap, thread-bare coveralls, and worn-out boots that he knew he couldn't afford to replace. After walking out to the road from the old tool shed that he used as a blind, he decided that he was done with hunting for good, just like that. Once Neil made up his mind to do something or not to do something, that was it. He quit smoking that way. He quit playing poker that way. And this cold, drizzly day, he decided to stop hunting.

In his seventies, I guess he had become tired of getting up before dawn to sit on a folding chair for hours waiting for a deer to show up, and also his reasons might have had something to do with unpleasant memories of the land. The days alone in the blind might have given him too much time to think about what had happened there during his boyhood—abandonment by his father, the long illness and death of his mother, and the struggles of subsistence living in a tin and tar paper shack with a dirt floor. He carried his rifle close to his body, cradled in his arms. The strap of an Army-green canvas bag hung over his wide sloping shoulders like a sack of memories.

As Neil made his way down the wet black road towards Irene Brown's house, he stopped mid-stride, and walked to the gate at Jordan Springs Cemetery where Laura, his mother, lay buried. She had died of breast cancer in the 1940s. As the sole caregiver for his mother, her long illness and death had flattened Neil's teenaged life like a bulldozer. He rested his gun on the cyclone fence, and stepped inside the grounds. He passed by the gravestones of long-dead, half-forgotten people that he had known during his life in Brown County, Texas. On the far side of a hundred-year-old oak tree, he removed his shapeless cap, and stood over his mother's grave. The face of the gravestone never changed. For him, it must have been like looking at a memory that couldn't be weathered away by rain or bleached out by the hot Texas sun.

Cold rain dripped on his thin gray hair, and ran down his forehead and neck. He fastened his top button, and pulled his bare hands into his coat sleeves. The air smelled of wood smoke. After about five minutes, he tapped the toe of his boot gently on his mother's flat gravestone, and returned to the road. Dogs barked from the ranches. Windmills groaned. Jack rabbits stood by the side of the road like marbled statues. Stella, his wife, and Irene Brown, the widow of Dennis, his best friend, waited down the road at Irene's house with hot coffee, ham and eggs, biscuits and gravy. Irene had stoked the kitchen fireplace with bone-dry mesquite. Struggling down a rainy country road towards people you love, warm food, hot coffee, and a bright fire made what Neil called a life. A cure for gray thoughts on a gray day.

After I married Neil's daughter, he gave me his scoped hunting rifle. Even though the stock had been beat up with use, the gun looked well-maintained. I could tell Neil was proud of his rifle.

"I've killed a lot of deer with this pump," Neil said. "I want you to have it, because my hunting days are over." He didn't feel the need to explain.

Other than shooting a twenty-two at scout camp when I was a young boy, I had never fired a gun. It pleased Laurene to see her father give me one of his most prized possessions. She wanted us to love each other. After a while, we did.

I took the rifle home to Grand Rapids, and didn't't give it another thought until a friend invited me to go hunting in Texas the following year. Laurene and I decided to fly down to Houston where she could stay with her parents while I hunted on a lease in the Texas

Hill Country. Neil and Stella were always happy to see their only daughter, and they seemed happy to see me, too. Stella had prepared chicken and dumplings for our evening meal. The steaming chicken broth smell made you want to gulp the thick air inside their tiny house. For dessert, Stella had baked a German Chocolate Cake, one of my favorites.

Neil's eyes lit up when I told him I had brought his deer rifle with me. As soon as we could be excused from the dinner table, we cleaned the gun together in the garage. Neil moved his hands gently over the stock like he was touching the arm of an old friend. After we finished with the gun, he rubbed the back of his neck with a bandana, and gave me some hunting tips while he looked out the garage door to the street. He had a faraway look in his eyes. From his quick sideways glances in my direction, I think he might have been bashful about giving me advice. Giving advice was something he rarely did. He had never had a father around to give him advice. And he never had a son to give advice. But there were a few things he wanted me to know.

"First thing I want to say about hunting is empty or not, think your gun's loaded, and think everyone else's gun's loaded—safety off and ready to shoot. If someone makes a mistake and points a gun barrel at you, drop to the dirt as quick as you can. You're gonnaf be better off embarrassed than dead. Second thing, never use the scope to look at a human being—that's what binoculars are for. Third, when you see a deer, the deer's gonna look much bigger through the scope than actual size. Make sure the antlers are outside the ears. Count the tines. People frown on shooting deer smaller than eight points.

"Another thing about scopes. Look behind your target to make sure there's nothing there. If you shoot a rancher's livestock, or worse than a cow, his favorite dog, he's gonna get real upset. You have no idea how upset. Why, you might see him dig two holes in the ground—one for the dead animal, and another one for you. I'm not foolin'. The last thing I want to say is to keep that scope away from your eyes. You've probably never heard of 'buck fever,' but 'buck fever' is when you get nervous after a big buck jumps out in front of you. You put the scope up against your eyeball and pull the trigger. You don't want to do that. That old Remington kicks like a rodeo horse. I know this, because it happened to me."

After a long pause, he added, "Now you needn't worry about getting a deer on your first hunt. Some people hunt their entire lives without getting a deer."

Laurene and I wanted to do something else while we were in Texas. For six months, Laurene had been concerned about a change in her left breast. Her gynecologist confirmed that she could also feel a textural difference close to the chest wall. In May 1991, Laurene met with a Grand Rapids oncologist who said he could find no evidence of disease, but he told her that she could return in a few months if she had further concerns. Laurene asked me to see if I could feel anything, but I couldn't. Nothing had appeared on a mammogram, and there had been no indications on a routine test the year before. The oncologist told Laurene not to worry. He told her that a preventative measure might be to change her diet by eating more plant-based foods, and giving up unhealthy foods like chocolate. The only unhealthy food she mentioned that I remember was chocolate, because I knew what would follow.

That was it for chocolate. Laurene made decisions like her father. The whole family had to stop eating chocolate, and any other food that Laurene deemed to be unhealthy. She cooked broccoli stir fries, and other vegetarian dishes. Our favorite snack foods were replaced by organic carrots and celery. The bars of "real" butter disappeared from our refrigerator. She threw away the leftover candy from Halloween, a hoard that I had stashed in the back of the pantry where I thought it would be safe. New fruit bowls decorated the kitchen counter, inviting us to eat apples, bananas, pineapples, and grapes, rather than cookies and ice cream. She purchased a blender that roared like a jet engine while it ingested fruits and veggies, and pulverized them into "green" smoothies that glowed on the counter top like some magical potion from a Harry Potter novel.

New cookbooks stood like scolding health foodies shouting slogans at us from the kitchen book shelves—"eat kale and you can't fail," "salads and beets are healthy treats." We stopped going out to dinner at restaurants heavy with fried-food menu items. I began to dream about hot juicy burgers and crisp onion rings loaded with salt and dripping with fat. I took advantage of lunch in the middle of the work day to satisfy my unhealthy food cravings. I packed emergency Snickers Bars in my briefcase. When alone in the kitchen, I stuffed the jet engine with scoops of ice cream, and squeezed heavy crisscrosses of chocolate syrup on top along with whole milk and powdered malt. Flipping the switch for a few seconds at 200 miles per hour produced a liquefied a shake with no more than a whisper of sound.

Our daughters concocted eating strategies of their own—for example, the Lucky Charms nutritional pitch:

"Mom, Lucky Charms are high in zinc."

"That's interesting, Meredith, how do you know?"

"It says so on the box! See, Mom." "How much sugar?"

"14 grams."

"Wow. That's a lot of sugar, Meredith."

"But Lucky Charms contains other healthy ingredients like *mayonnaise*."

"You mean *manganese*."

Laurene loved rules to order one's life, and when she made a new rule, we all had to get in line. Further, Laurene believed that if you followed the rules, life would be fair to everyone and all would be well. Her parents had raised to her to follow rules covering every aspect of daily living. Rather than ten commandments, there were hundreds. Laurene told me that when she was a young girl, she would argue with Neil and Stella about changing the rules, but she would never break rules on her own. She loved to argue, and since she was the only child, she argued most of the time with her parents, her father more than her mother. Neil once told her when she was a teenager, "Laurene, if you argue with people like you argue with me, no one will ever like you."

Laurene made another appointment in August 1991, and again, the oncologist observed nothing. She returned in October, and finally, the doctor noted a difference in her left breast. He still said there was no cause for alarm. We wanted a second opinion, but at first, he first refused to write a letter. He looked up at us from the paperwork on his desk as if we were making a lot of trouble over nothing. When we pushed back, he reluctantly wrote a referral letter to MD Anderson in

Houston. The last line of the letter read: "I don't feel this is a malignancy, but it should be biopsied to make sure."

To this day, the doctor's letter rests at the bottom of Laurene's permanent medical file at MD Anderson (*Patient #114148*). During the next ten years, I would often ferry her file from one appointment to the next to expedite an appointment. After ten years, I had to move the records around the clinic in a wheelchair. The file had grown to three feet high, held together with binder clips and rubber bands; filled with blood work reports, doctor's clinic notes, radiologists' reports, imaging results from CT and MRI scans, medications and dosages, weight, temperature, and blood pressure readings. Today scanners digitize more of the details, and keep the dog-eared, ragged paper trail neatly hidden in computer memory.

We made an appointment at MD Anderson for the Monday after my weekend hunt—November 6, 1991. On the sunny fall day before the appointment, Neil, Stella, and Laurene picked me up at a gas station where my hunting buddies had dropped me off near Johnson City.

Neil stuck his head out of the car window, and said, "Howdy...did you get your buck?"

His blue eyes brightened and he laughed with his entire body when I told him that I had taken two bucks with his rifle. He kept saying, *"Two bucks, two bucks!"* I sat in the back seat of his blue Chevy Impala with Laurene, and apologized to everyone because I stunk. Laurene wanted to know about the red crescent wound beneath my purple right eye. Contrary to Neil's warnings, when the first buck jumped out from behind a pile of brush, I placed the scope against my eye and pulled the trigger. Just like that! Blood spewed all over my clothes and onto the ground. I thought, *Did the deer in Texas shoot back?*

Neil talked freely in the car, something he rarely did. He jabbered about how he had been to Canada, and had hunted birds in South Dakota, but had never been to Michigan. With a twinkle in her eyes, Stella added that when the Canadian border guard asked Neil for his country of origin, he replied, "Texas." Stella had been mortified. Neil questioned me about the weather in Michigan, and the hunting and fishing. He exhausted his knowledge of Michigan by telling about his general practitioner. "My doctor grew up in a town called Kalkaska, Michigan—*'three 'A's' and three 'K's,'*" he said slowly and repeated, *"three 'A's' and three 'K's'— Kalkaska, Michigan. How 'bout that?"*

I asked Neil why they had moved from Brownwood to Houston soon after Laurene's birth.

"We wanted a better life. I didn't want to stay somewhere that was going nowhere. After the war, there were plenty of good-paying jobs in Houston. With

Stella's teaching and my job with the city, we bought a house and paid for Laurene to go to college. I paid that house off in four years, because I couldn't stand the mortgage hanging over our heads. We could've been happy in Brownwood, but we did better for ourselves in Houston. Until a while ago, we kept a small apartment in Brownwood for spending weekends with our old friends. We hunted on Saturday mornings, danced on Saturday nights, and drove home after church on Sundays. Laurene went along. I expect we made the best of two worlds."

Neil entertained us with stories of Laurene's childhood, and about his friends in Brownwood. He talked about his only trip to Europe. Dennis and Irene had traveled with them, and Dennis had teased Neil for bringing canned goods to Paris. Neil justified himself by saying that he didn't know what the food would be like over there, so he had packed a few cans of red beans for an emergency. He also told us that after Stella and he were married, Dennis and Irene accompanied them on their honeymoon trip to "Old Mexico." Over the five-hour drive, Neil, Stella, and Laurene gave me an extensive history of their family and friends, and the stories behind each of them. I could tell how absorbed this small family was in the lives of the people they loved.

Halfway back to Houston, we stopped for barbecue in Brenham, Texas. The menu on the wall listed nearly all of Laurene's forbidden foods in one large display behind the long counter. The menu described a range of combinations that excited me beyond description: *"BAR-B-Q BEEF, BAR-B-Q SPARE RIBS, CHOPPED BAR-B-Q BEEF, BAR-B-Q GERMAN SAUSAGE, BAR-B-Q CHICKEN, CHICKEN FRIED STEAK, FRIED SHRIMP, BQ SAUCE, HOT ROLLS, RED BEANS, POTATO SALAD, GREEN BEANS, MASHED POTATOES, COLESLAW, CORN, CARROTS, BLACKBERRY, CHERRY, PEACH COBBLER, BANANA PUDDING, SWEET TEA, AND DR PEPPER.*

At hunting camp, I had started each day two hours before first light with a long walk to a brush blind. In my backpack, I had two cans of Coke and two apples to last me until an hour after sundown. Now, I ordered sliced beef with pickles, onions and jalapeños on bread with extra barbecue sauce, beans, cole slaw, and sweetened ice tea. Behind the counter, a young man who held a long flat-nosed knife sliced a long slab of smoked beef ribboned with fat. (I'm not done telling you about this meal.) For dessert, I had blackberry cobbler topped with Bluebell Ice Cream. Laurene gave me a spoonful of her banana pudding. I remember how happy we all were. No one talked about the appointment the following morning.

When Laurene objected to my extensive food order, Neil defended me: "I've been eating like this my entire life, and I'm doing just fine. Besides, Randy killed his first deer. We need to celebrate!" Shooting your first deer in Texas is a big deal like in a lot of places, but I suppose in Texas it's a bigger deal like everything else there.

After lunch, Laurene and I traded seats with Neil and Stella. I took the wheel, and drove the rest of the way back to Houston. We traversed three of Texas' geographic regions: the rolling plains of Central Texas, the Hill Country around Austin, and as we approached Houston, the Gulf Coastal Plain. From the 610 Loop we could see the skyline and the urban core of Houston, our next day's destination. I reached for Laurene's hand. I began to worry. *What tests will they do? How long before we see the results? What if Laurene has cancer? How will she react? I need to find a pen and notepad. I'll take notes. She looks so healthy. She's too young to have cancer. She follows all the rules of healthy living.*

It was half dark when we pulled into the driveway. Seed carriers from the neighbor's box elders helicoptered over the concrete. Neil's camper-topped red pickup rested at an odd angle outside the garage, sporting a flat tire.
"I need to sell that truck," he said. A week later, he sold his truck. Just like that.

"Daddy's getting older," Laurene said. "I can't believe he decided to give up hunting. I can't believe he's selling his truck.

Randy Evans

Lesson One

It doesn't matter how good you happen to be, or how well you follow the rules. Bad things can happen. There is no limit to how many bad things can happen.

2.

Not an uncommon occurrence. It makes even
The well-intended scurry like an animal
Who sees a monster in the margin of his nightmare.

Dante's Inferno, Canto II

We had been in the hospital for less than two hours on the following Monday morning. Technicians and nurses had administered an ultrasound and fine-needle aspiration of the breast. After they numbed her breast with local anesthetic, Laurene said that she only felt pressure. Twenty minutes later, a nurse told us to make another appointment for the same day. Since it had taken weeks to schedule the tests, the short interval until the next appointment frightened us. Why the urgency?

While Laurene was getting dressed, I chased the nurse down in the hallway. She wouldn't tell me what she knew, but I could tell from the way she turned her face away from me that this was not going to be a good day.

The hours before the afternoon appointment dragged. We drove back to Neil and Stella's house, and spread a blanket out in the backyard. I can't remember what we talked about, but it wasn't about cancer. We might have talked about fire ants when one stung me, or about Neil's prolific okra garden with stalks that grew above the wood-slatted fence along the side of the house. At one point, Neil came into the backyard and trimmed some okra with his slender pocket knife. "For dinner," he said in a raspy voice. He walked back inside bent forward as though he was carrying an invisible bag on his back. I could tell he was worried. He looked like a walking question mark. When we came back inside the house, we found Stella attacking the kitchen floor with her broom, her arthritic hands wrapped around the broom handle like claws with the thumb of her left hand lower and pointed towards the floor.

Returning to MD Anderson in the afternoon, I dropped Laurene off at the entrance and drove off to park the car. I was driving Neil and Stella's car, so I looked for a wide space on the roof deck of the garage. When I approached the clinic building, I passed a dozen patients sitting outside smoking, hunched over men hooked up to IV stands like old chairs sitting next to floor lamps. A year later, the clinic would ban smoking on the premises, but I remember those emaciated men puffing away, and my thoughts at the time. *They had brought cancer on themselves. It was their fault. You'd think they'd have had enough sense to stop smoking. Laurene didn't smoke and she didn't drink. She had led a healthy life. She had always been a good person. She had followed the rules. She could not have cancer. It would not be fair.*

MD Anderson sprawls across 25 buildings covering 14 million square feet on more than seven acres, including an inpatient pavilion with 507 beds, five research buildings, three outpatient clinic buildings, two faculty office buildings, a proton radiation clinic building, and a patient-family hotel. MD Anderson's 20,000-plus cancer fighters treat more than 100,000 patients per year. Inside the outpatient clinics, you have the feel of a busy international airport with people of all ages and nationalities—Arab women wearing burqas and tunics, Hasidic Jewish men with long beards and skull caps. You can pick up accents from faraway regions, like all the species of birds in the world are chirping at once, the song of each entering the songs of the others.

Even though it was November, Christmas cards created by children cancer patients through the Children's Art Project were for sale in the lobby, as well as sparkling Christopher Radko glass-blown tree ornaments. The clinic impressed me as an upbeat place of hope, a mix of disabled and able-bodied people moving around with purpose—fifteen thousand outpatient visits a day. I passed through the vast clinic lobby and found the correct elevator (Elevator B).

When I arrived at the radiation clinic waiting room, Laurene sat reading a book with great intensity. She always read when she wanted to get her mind off something. Her feet were tucked under the rest of her body like she always did when she was reading. The receptionist gave us a nod within fifteen minutes. At the time, I could not appreciate that fifteen minutes was a lightning-fast wait time for a cancer appointment. On "clinic days," oncologists would often meet with fifteen or more patients. Some visits took a few minutes; others lasted up to an hour. It depended on what was happening with the patient. Good news. Bad news. No news.

A young radiologist in a white lab coat didn't hesitate to tell us what we had to hear. Laurene had cancer. The doctor told us what he knew so far. The biopsy had revealed a high grade tumor (high grade refers to the aggressiveness of the tumor). The diagnosis was breast cancer (later on a pathologist who looked at the biopsy gave us a more specific diagnosis: invasive ductal carcinoma). The doctor told us that the staging, although tentative, was not the worst news we could have received, but not good news. I felt blood flushing my face.

The TNM staging system (T=tumor, N=nodes, and M=metastasis), indicated stage 3 cancer (T3,N1, M0). At last, we knew more about what we were dealing with. T3 referred to the size of the tumor (1cm =.39 inches), and the doctor was guessing that the tumor in Laurene's left breast was more than 5 centimeters. I did the math—about two inches. N1 meant that positive lymph nodes were most likely present. M0 indicated that further testing would be required to make sure that the cancer had not metastasized to other parts of the body, since the initial diagnosis had been based on a microscopic view of the breast cells aspirated by the biopsy.

Damn that doctor in Grand Rapids! What he had failed to identify over a six-month period, MD Anderson had identified in a few minutes, or at least, in a few hours.

I held Laurene's hand. I was blown away by the news. I felt as though a monster had entered the room. I wanted to run away; scurry for cover. I didn't want to be there. This couldn't be happening. My eyes blurred. The objects in the room seemed out of scale. The room appeared overly small for such enormous news, a *roomette* rather than a room. We were sitting in this miniature-sized living room. The chairs and table seemed too small. The lamp looked too small for the table. The inspirational posters on the walls shouted messages that were out of place in this setting. Unlike the smallish furniture, the posters appeared as large as billboards on a highway: *"CANCER IS A WORD NOT A SENTENCE," "CANCER CANNOT EAT AWAY PEACE," "LOVE IS BETTER THAN ANGER," "MAMMOGRAPHY SAVES LIVES."*

This must be the bad news room. Are we supposed to read the posters, and think that everything is okay? They have staged this room to look like someone's living room. Living room. Ha! I don't like this room, and I don't like this doctor. His lab coat with his name embroidered on the front makes him look like a garage mechanic.

Other than my grandfather, cancer had never raised its ugly head in my immediate family. Cancer happened to acquaintances or strangers, but not to someone close. Not to my parents or my children or my wife. Our second marriage had just begun four years earlier. What would happen to us? Our children? I slouched down in the tiny chair. *Look at Laurene! She's doing better than me. I'm leaning back and she's leaning forward. She's leaning into the news. She's clear-eyed. She's not zoning out like me. She wants to know the new set of rules so she can challenge them. She's making the doctor sweat under his white lab coat. She's asking so many questions! I was thinking what Neil had said to Laurene when she was a teenager. If you ask the doctor too many questions, he won't like you.*

Laurene acted like she was in GE business meeting. She didn't care to charm the doctor. She didn't care about how much he liked her. She wanted to know as much as she could about the pathology report. How invasive was the cancer? What other tests would be performed? What did the blood work show? How would we know if the cancer had spread beyond her chest? Where might it travel—to the other breast or somewhere else? Her mind operated in "think" mode— no time for emotions. She wanted facts. The oncologist could only tell us that the cancer was "locally advanced." He said, "It's bad, but not as bad as it could be." Laurene asked about staging. The doctor said that the pathologist had graded the cancer Stage IIB (the tumor was less than 5 centimeters with no evidence that the cancer had spread to auxiliary lymph nodes).

When the doctor started to leave, Laurene blocked the door. I wanted to laugh, because the doctor had no idea who he was dealing with. He had lost control of the meeting. Laurene had more questions. The doctor sat back down. The doctor stopped sweating. His face muscles relaxed. I think he had realized that he would be unable to leave until Laurene was through with him, so he might as well relax. We discussed treatment options and next steps. When Laurene asked what we could do now, we were not expecting his answer. We thought that he might tell us about how we could be better informed, or outline alternative approaches to control the cancer in addition to medical treatment. Instead, he said to pay attention to our marriage relationship. Based on his experience, he said that dealing with cancer strains marriages. We assured him that we could handle cancer like we had dealt with other life challenges— like raising a blended family, balancing our work schedules, and caring for our parents.

I resented his comments. *Are you a psychologist? So one doctor tells us not to eat chocolate, and this one wants us to go to marriage counseling.*

Rather than discounting what she had heard from the doctor like I had, Laurene looked for ways to benefit from his advice. She got it immediately—cancer involved more than medical issues. Living with cancer involved substantial quality of life issues. As we headed back to the lobby, she began to form mental action plans. Her first thoughts focused on me and the family. She didn't want the disease to affect my work or the girls' school performance. She could quit her job and stay with her parents for treatments, if I could manage work and take care of the girls while she was away. She said that she was out of shape spiritually, and needed to do some work on her faith. She needed access to the latest new developments in breast oncology. She needed to join a support group, and maybe find a counselor. She wanted a new oncologist in Grand Rapids to backup her new doctors in Houston. We needed to revise our family budget without her income, and cut our expenses, and review our health care plans. Laurene knew that cancer was a big deal, before I did.

As we walked down the hallway towards Elevator B, I could see her change. Her blue almond-shaped eyes turned a shade darker. Her face muscles tensed with resolve. She was going to beat the cancer. "We can do this," she said. "You get the car. I'm going to buy Christmas ornaments for the girls." As I exited the building, I looked back at her. Her tall body bent over the display tables of ornaments. Her light brown hair hung over her face. She was a good-looking woman.

The lost souls still sat on the concrete wall as I walked out of the clinic to the parking garage. They resembled paper-thin zombies appearing and disappearing in smoke clouds. One man tapped a cigarette from his pack of Camels. When he wrapped his thin fingers around the cigarette and lit up, the pulsing embers looked as if they measured out the residual life still inside his frail body.

The man reminded me of my grandfather who had smoked unfiltered Camels. He had started his smoking career at age 14 as a Pennsylvania coal miner. At some time in his life, he had had his forearm tattooed with the tobacco company's iconic one-humped camel. (The smoky clouds from the cancer patients smelled like my grandfather.) Then one day soon after I was born, he stopped smoking and swearing—just like Neil had stopped smoking and playing poker. But my grandfather quit too late. He developed lung cancer in his seventies when I was in my thirties. We sat on his screened-in patio eating my grandmother's pickled relish on a slice of white bread while he talked to me about how the brakes in cars had improved during his lifetime. He referred to the moon landing. He gave me advice to live by. The advice I remember—bend your knees when you lift, don't shovel snow with the shovel handle pointed at your privates, keep your shoes shined, and never join a church with a building campaign.

That my loving grandfather was dying of a strange disease was about all I knew at the time. Other than a great aunt who had died of breast cancer, there was no history of cancer in my family. I could only observe my grandfather's labored breathing as he lay in bed propped up by pillows. I was spared seeing his pain, and knew nothing of his fear and anxiety over the disease, but I first used the word "cancer" as the name for the disease that had killed my grandfather. *Would I lose Laurene like I had lost him, or could we beat this? How long would we need to deal with this unwanted intrusion into our busy lives? How could I take care of the kids and work while Laurene went through radiation and chemotherapy?*

I didn't know much more about cancer at age forty-five than I had known from taking high school biology. I had no idea what caused cancer, how it spread from one site in the body to another, or how it could crowd out healthy cells, and, too often, kill people. For weeks after Laurene's diagnosis, I listened to how people used the word "cancer" in everyday life. A newscaster on the TV said, "Extreme groups are spreading like cancer." Another day, I heard "Radical ideologies are metastasizing." "Evil predator," "ruthless," "invasive," "intractable," and "mysterious" were the words used to portray cancer as an agent of death invested with magical powers. A life-threatening disease had inflated into a monster in my mind, one who was about to carry my wife away.

Laurene didn't seem to feel the same way about cancer. If she harbored exaggerated fears similar to mine about the disease, she didn't share them with me. That we were beginning a long and difficult journey did not occur to me at the time. I had no clue that I was entering a stage of my life comparable to an all-consuming inferno. More than a bump in the road. A big deal.

Randy Evans

Lesson Two

People form crazy abstractions about cancer that we would never ascribe to the common cold or to the flu.

3.

At that, the pitch-dark plain shook.
Every aspect of that moment is burned in my brain:
The cold sweat inside my clothes.

Dante's Inferno, Canto III

On the way back to Neil and Stella's house, we watched people speed by on their way home from work. High billboards and neon signs shouted advertising messages at us like *Gallery Furniture Saves You Money!*—the slogan of a local businessman who held a fistful of cash over his larger-than-life head. The whole world seemed out-of-scale, from the miniature conference room at MD Anderson where we had received the bad news, to the furniture magnate on the billboard with his yard-wide fake smile. *Too small or too big. Out of the ordinary. No text for what we needed to do. Just large letters on large billboards.*

We turned off the 610 Loop, and took the familiar turns to Neil and Stella's. Laurene remarked about how the neighborhood had both changed and remained the same since her girlhood. All the homes on the street were about the same size, one-story brick ranch houses built in the 50s. Neil and Stella's first home had been their last home. Laurene pointed out a Korean Methodist Church, a new community center, a strip mall with a video store, the favorite swing swaying on rusty chains in a rundown park, and a Texas-style

French restaurant that Laurene said displayed exotic game mounts on the inside walls. We pulled into the driveway of the tiny bungalow behind Neil's red pickup. I looked over at Laurene to see dried-up tear tracks on her face. She rubbed her eyes and pulled back her hair as she opened the screen door. I could tell that she was steeling herself to face her parents with the news. The wind was beginning to blow, and the screen door slammed behind her. I opened the door, and the door slammed again.

Laurene and I found Neil and Stella in the family room watching an old episode of Lawrence Welk. When Laurene informed them of her diagnosis, they both cried while an accordion player squeezed out a tune from the TV. The news upset Neil beyond anything I had ever seen from him. Perhaps life-long anxiety about Laurene's inherited risk surfaced. I'm sure he remembered the pain and suffering that his mother had endured. He may have thought about how hard it had been to care for his mother with no help. Until she died, Neil had raised turkeys on the small farm. He had to chase them down in order to sell them in Brownwood. He would drive the turkeys to town in an old jalopy. At the time, there was no road access, so he had to drive over fields and through gates to get to the road. He had also worked in town at a bakery while going to school. Taking care of his mother had not been easy. For perhaps all of these reasons, and the fact that he loved his daughter more than anything, his hard face softened in a sorrowful way. He fell into silence.

The big band played on the TV: *"Good night sweetheart, till we meet tomorrow, Good night sweetheart, sleep will banish sorrow..."*

After we watched the evening news with Neil and Stella, they retired to bed with hugs and kisses for both of us. They still looked stunned. Laurene and I were too hyped to sleep, so we laid together in her bed. Her room had not changed since high school. The pink, frilly bedspread and hot pink cushions remained, the same drapes, lamps, nightstands, and a double bed with springs that creaked every time you made the slightest movement. In the small house the two bedrooms were separated by a tiny bathroom. We were literally less than ten feet from Neil and Stella. We could hear them snore.

It was useless to try to sleep. As we had done in the afternoon of this long day, we decided to take a blanket to the backyard. We placed it near the high stalks of Neil's okra garden where the tall plants hung over us like tassels. I could smell the moist evening air and a faint scent of Laurene's perfume. We rested on our backs and watched the stars in silence. The face of the night sky dwarfed the little house in the little yard. It made me think of the lyrics, *the stars at night are big and bright, deep in the heart of Texas.* What was deep in my heart at this moment? Like the night sky, my heart contained boundless details with no specificity. All the thoughts were bumping against each other. Laurene leaned into my side, and splayed her left leg over my right leg. A soft wind blew her hair in my face. Laying on the blanket beside my wife, her face splashed by moonlight, I forgot for a moment about the cancer cells hidden under her skin.

We lay still next to each other for a longtime until I heard tapping sounds moving from place to place on the other side of the high wooden fence that enclosed the yard. What I first thought were dead leaves stirred by the wind, sounded nervous and hostile. ***"RATS!"*** Laurene said. I didn't bother to wait for her. I grabbed the blanket, and leapt towards the house. Laurene laughed at my quick exit.

"You run like a damn Yankee!" she said. She knew I was skittish about all the creepy, crawly creatures in Texas.

Once inside, Laurene removed two old jelly jars from a shelf in the kitchen, and handed me one. I was in a cold sweat.

"Momma and Daddy never throw anything away," she said.

On my jar, I could see the nearly washed out music bars of "My Old Kentucky Home" etched on the glass: "eep no more, m lady...weep no more today" Laurene poured stiff shots of Maker's Mark into the jelly jars. The whiskey warmed me. We sat down in the family room that Neil had built in the sixties so Laurene could have parties with her friends. Around the room you could see a gun cabinet, a large deer mount, a window air conditioner, and a "Dad of the Year" plaque that Neil had received from Laurene's sorority at Sam Houston State. After a few sips, Laurene wanted to talk.

"I am so sorry you have to deal with this. We just got married a few years ago."

"I'm glad you decided to marry me."

"I hope your girls know how much I love them."

"We all love each other."

"I'm not used to being sick. I might get ornery."

"I doubt that will happen...but you can be ornery. I won't mind."

"Don't leave me."

"I won't leave you."

We had dated for three years before our marriage; a long time from my perspective. Laurene had wanted a guarantee that our marriage would work. She didn't want to make a mistake about us. We had both been divorced after fifteen-year first marriages. One morning, I ran across a woman from church in the supermarket who told me that Laurene had called her to do a reference check on me. I thought, *how many women do reference checks on prospective husbands?* The woman wanted me to know that she had given me a thumbs up. She examined a cantaloupe in the produce aisle—pressing the skin, smelling the stem. She lifted the melon up and down as she spoke with an accent that reminded me of Laurene's.

"Don't worry, Laurene will get off the fence sooner or later. My husband says she's too intense, but I don't see her that way. She's a hard-working woman raising those two girls, holding down a job, and going back to school. I remember when John and she broke up. She jogged through the neighborhood every day crying her eyes out. She looked thin as a scarecrow. Did you know I grew up in Texas, too? I brought her a bottle of Jack Daniels after John left. She invited me in for a drink, which I expected she would. She drinks whiskey and coke...Texans do that. By the way, if you plan on marrying a Texan, you better learn to dance the two-step. I think it's a good sign when a woman drinks whiskey, don't you? You're a strong man. You need a strong woman. Texas produces strong women like Laurene and me. My husband asked me why Texan women are so strong, and I told him *because of asshole Texas men*...but in all fairness, there are asshole men everywhere...not *you* of course." She pointed the stem end of the cantaloupe in my direction like it was her prop for an asshole.

Laurene would say, "I want you to know the *real* me. I want you to know about all my faults. I want you to know every rotten part of me." She absolutely refused for me to idealize her. Maybe she knew me better than I knew myself—how I idealized women. Of course, the flip side of this conversation was that she wanted to know every "rotten part of *me*" as well. I told her that I lived in an introverted bubble, that I spent most of my time unaware of my surroundings, that I had difficulty doing more than one thing at a time. I told her that I was impatient, and often made decisions impulsively, that my feelings were easily hurt, and that I was too ambitious about my career to live a balanced life. (I didn't tell her the really bad stuff.)

I had no idea how to close the deal with her. After three years, I had begun to think about moving on. I began to think that I could find someone else who would be less difficult to win over, maybe someone a bit more easygoing. Then one evening I said, "Laurene, I can't give you the kind of guarantee you want. There are no guarantees. You need to make a decision." I could almost hear her thinking, *I want a guarantee that our marriage will work and we'll be together forever. He won't give me a guarantee, but I know he loves me. Can I live with that? Yes. I guess we should get married before he gets tired of waiting and dumps me.*

She had the practical mind of her father.

A month later we were engaged in the dining room of a Tudor mansion that had been turned into a supper club. We met after work. That day, Laurene had given a product planning presentation on a new GE lighting product. She wanted to talk about work for a while to clear her mind. She knew what I was about to do, but she wanted to get everything else off her chest. I proposed, and she said yes. I slipped a sapphire and diamond wedding ring on her finger. After several visits to a local jeweler, he had designed the ring to Laurene's specifications. She had wanted a sapphire ring that looked like Princess Diana's. She knew what she wanted, and did not like surprises. That night she brought her Polaroid camera along. Pictures preceded kisses.

During our engagement, Laurene signed us up for pre-marital counseling. We enrolled in a workshop titled "Stepping into Step Parenting." A psychologist administered batteries of inventories. We discovered that our two personality types couldn't have been more different; we were what Carl Jung had named "Dionysian opposites." Laurene was an extrovert. I was an introvert. Laurene made decisions based on facts. I made gut-based decisions. Laurene used her mind to solve problems. I solved problems based on feelings and values. Laurene liked to plan the future in detail. I preferred to let things happen.

Wedding planning proved to be the first test of our significant style differences. We met every night after work to go over the invitation list, the wedding attendants, the photographer, the food and entertainment. She wanted a preacher friend to perform the service, but she wanted to write out what he would say and limit his time. We listened to tapes from local musicians, and settled on a harpist. She wanted the girls to wear identical outfits with matching white and pink hats, dresses, stockings, and shoes. We ordered both a white cake and a dark "groom's cake," a Southern tradition: I wanted German chocolate. What if our outdoor wedding was rained out? We needed a backup plan. The details seemed to be endless, and I would often cut off our weeknight meetings by eleven.

During the months before the wedding, I also had to pass muster with Laurene's entire family: Jennifer and Meredith, my future stepchildren; her parents, Neil and Stella; Laurene's aunts and uncles and cousins from Texas, including her Uncle William Rice who had spent his life bull riding on the rodeo circuit.

When I first met Uncle Rice and Laurene's cousins, Bo and Billy Don, we sat in the family room with Neil while Laurene, Stella, and the other women removed dove filets from milk cartons, dipped them in milk, egg, and flour, and began to batter fry them on the stove in a cast iron skillet. No one said a word for a long time. I noticed that I was the only one sitting there without a big belt buckle and Western boots. There was no TV playing, or anything else to distract us from sizing each other up. Everyone held a tumbler of iced tea. Nothing to nibble on other than some unshelled pecans. Finally, after what seemed years, Billy Don half-turned to me, careful not to make eye contact.

"Shoot birds?"

"No, I've never shot a bird."

(Long Pause)

"We do."

I don't know how it happened, but they all decided they liked me. At least they didn't take as long as Laurene had. Billy Don and his family ended up supporting Laurene and me in many different ways over the next ten years.

We married on September 5, 1987. Amy and Laura, my two daughters, along with Jennifer and Meredith, wore frilly pink bridesmaid dresses along with white hats, white stockings, and white shoes. They each carried a bouquet of pink flowers while the harpist played the Pachelbel Canon in D. The preacher read his scripted sermon with only a few additional anecdotes. At the time, Amy and Laura were 13 and 11; Jennifer and Meredith, were 10 and 6. Meredith had to be pried from her mother's arms, as we left the reception. She sobbed uncontrollably. She had never been away from Laurene before.

Laurene had left the details of the honeymoon to me. I was thrilled that she would delegate our honeymoon trip to me. How uncharacteristic of her. "Surprise me!," she said. Boy, would she regret it.

When we arrived in Zurich the day after the wedding, Laurene asked me for the itinerary. I told her that I had made reservations for the first night, and rented a Fiat for two weeks. There was no itinerary. She looked surprised, but not pleased.

I thought that we might cross the Alps like Hannibal, and roam around Italy for a few weeks. Unfortunately, I had rented a car in Switzerland that required unleaded fuel. When we crossed the border into Italy, we were provided with a map showing six Agip Stations with unleaded fuel in the entire country. When we arrived at the first station with its yellow, black, and red dragon logo, Laurene jumped out of the car with her dictionary, and towered over a short Italian gas attendant. He looked up at her with horror like this tall American woman was about to attack him.

"S*enza piombo?*" Laurene shouted with her head pointed at the phrase section of the tiny dictionary.

"*No, no, senza piombo.*" The man raised his arms skyward, as though he was searching for divine protection.

They were out of unleaded gas. We did find gas later in the day, and stopped at a bank for *lire*. Gas, cash, and a place to sleep were Laurene's priorities until she settled down, and we started to have fun. Over the next two weeks, we stayed in all manner of lodging, from an estate home in Lucca with satin wallpaper, chandeliers and marble-walled showers, to a room in Padua with unpainted walls, peeling plaster, a bare light bulb hanging from the ceiling, and a shared bathroom down the hall.

Our honeymoon ended in an odd way. We received a call from Laurene's boss at GE. He wanted her to attend a product marketing meeting in Paris on the day she had been scheduled to return to work. He said that the company would pay for her return air fare, rescheduling penalties, and expenses, if she could rearrange her return trip. So on the final day of a romantic two-week romp through Europe, Laurene flew from Milan to Paris, and I flew from Milan to Cleveland. No one was more surprised than our girls when I arrived home without their mother.

A week later, Laurene returned home, probably the only GE employee to ever be reimbursed for a honeymoon trip. Neil and Stella had been our babysitters, and they stayed on to help me out until Laurene returned.

"That was an awful lot to ask," Neil said, referring to Laurene's boss. "How in the heck did he find you?"

Laurene planned our future trips. Over the following years, we would load the kids in the car or book flights for what Laurene called their "educational vacations." Laurene wanted "the girls" to see the country: Boston, Chicago, Hawaii, Houston, New York City, Baltimore, Philadelphia, Washington, DC, and Williamsburg, Virginia, among others, whether they wanted to or not.

Laurene would read about what we were to see while I drove the car. The girls wanted to buy trinkets in souvenir shops, and a constant stream of complaints issued from the back seat, the most common one—"Jennifer's knees are sticking to my knees!" Once, Meredith passed her mother a note predicting that she would soon have a fit. Laurene responded by writing her a brief inquiry about when and where she intended to have her fit. Meredith replied that she would wait until we had arrived home, because the backseat was too crowded for a proper fit. Later, Meredith changed her mind, and informed Laurene that she was going to jump out of the car window, but she never did. Instead, she turned herself upside down, and through the rear view mirror, I could see her walking off the ceiling of the car with her pink Roger Rabbit high tops.

No matter what the complaints, Laurene dragged us from one museum and historical marker to another from North to South and from one Coast to the other. Determined that the girls would grow up well-educated and well-traveled, Laurene never gave up wanting to see the world along with her family. Staying around home was her father's idea of a good life, and my father would agree. They had seen enough of the world during WWII. Wars do that to people. But for Laurene, new places were like wrapped gifts to be opened with curiosity and delight, something she could do for the people she loved.

The guarantee that our life together would work was something I couldn't give Laurene before our marriage, but when she asked me not to leave her after the cancer diagnosis, I gave her a promise that I could keep and wanted to keep.

Lesson Three

When you see a clear sky, a smooth ribbon of highway ahead, and think you will keep going on and on past the horizon, all of a sudden there is no sky, no road, and no horizon. You are lost without a map.

4.

*...hearing this saddened me; I could clearly see
There were many here of great worth,
Suspended in Limbo between better and worse.*

Dante's Inferno, Canto IV

Early evening the next day, we met a kind, intelligent woman whom Laurene had contacted for information about support group meetings. She unlocked the door to "The Rose," a mammography facility on Stella Link Road, so we could prepare for the next day's appointment with Laurene's primary oncologist. She also lent us a tape recorder to record our conversation with the doctor. Laurene thanked her for lending a tape recorder to a perfect stranger. She promised to return it.

The facility also served as the site for "Rosebuds," a support group that Laurene would later join. Rosebuds had a tall file filled with tons of information not yet available on the Internet.

Laurene looked through the file cabinet, drawer by drawer. She didn't want to miss anything. The dedicated support group room contained wigs, prostheses, and pictures of the support group members. We stayed until after midnight, looking at clinical trial information, survival statistics, and treatment options. We became thoroughly tired and confused. This was the first of many evenings and nights that I would spend in buildings at or near the Texas Medical Center, often trying to catch some sleep despite the pounding jackhammers, persistently opening space for new buildings to fight cancer.

The following day, Laurene met with her oncologist. After expressing frustration about not knowing what to do, she said, "I need you to be my advocate." He gave her a hug and said he would. Over the following decade, he consistently treated her as a woman first—a woman who happened to have breast cancer. He would begin each appointment by asking Laurene for her questions, but I could tell that his examination had begun as soon as we walked through his door. He observed how Laurene expressed herself, her tone of voice, the movement of her body. I took careful notes. Sometimes I had questions, too, and the doctor also listened to me, answering my questions. I always felt that we were part of a team. Getting directly involved in her survival remained a constant for the next ten plus years.

Laurene wanted information, even when the news wasn't positive. She asked so many questions, that we began to call them "Laurene questions." Her brand of questioning was sincere, succinct, appropriate, and always polite. If the answers didn't satisfy her, she asked follow-up questions. Her tone of voice was calm and unthreatening, not a hint of underlying emotion or a bit of sarcasm. In spite of her father's concern that people wouldn't like Laurene if she argued too much or asked too many questions, people liked and even loved her. But her questions were unrelenting:

How many treatments will I have?
How long will each treatment take?
Will the drugs be administered by IV?
Should I eat before treatment? After treatment?
Can I take my regular medications?
What side effects are there?
How can the side effects be treated?
Will the side effects get better or worse during treatment?
Can I still walk and ride my bike?
Will I lose my hair right away?
Would you give me your daytime phone number? Your night number?
Do you have a beeper?

As a product manager at GE, attention to detail had been Laurene's strength. She absorbed facts from all facets of life, including popular culture. She knew more about sports than most men, and could trade opinions with the most avid sports fanatic. She didn't read the sports pages for fun. She regarded knowing about sports as a career strategy in a male-dominated company. Her ability to absorb facts extended beyond sports. She liked history, especially Texas history. She could name all 254 counties in Texas. One year, Laurene brought us to San Antonio where she toured us through the Alamo like a history professor taking her students on a field trip.

Laurene also knew how to get things done outside the system. From the cafeteria to the pharmacy to physical therapy to appointment scheduling to the billing department, people wanted to assist her, or assist me on her behalf. She charmed people. The staff helped everyone, but they helped her a bit more. She knew that people could help her. "The nurses are the key," she said. "Doctors are important, but nurses will answer questions the doctors can't or won't." She absorbed hundreds of names at the clinic, and more than names, she knew who people were dating, what they were studying in school, and where they grew up. When we were at home, I often overheard Laurene counseling with staff from the hospital on the telephone about everything from how to break up with a boyfriend to how to buy a car or a house.

And when she couldn't charm people, she begged. "You have to know how to beg," she told me. "No one should be above begging."

The breast oncology team recommended a delay in surgery to see if the tumor could first be reduced in size through chemotherapy and radiation. Unconventional at the time, Laurene's case had to be presented to an Institutional Review Board. Laurene sat behind a curtain in the back of a conference room, while a panel of doctors discussed her case. She wore a hospital gown in the event one of the doctors wanted to examine her. She could hear all the deliberations. Like a jury, they reached a verdict. The doctors approved the proposed protocol, one that would later become a standard treatment option. Lopping off a woman's breasts had most often been the first procedure, rather than second, third, or not at all.

Laurene's treatment began in December 1991 with neoadjuvant chemotherapy (FAC), a concoction of three powerful drugs: 5-fluoroucil (5FU), doxorubicin (Adriamycin), and cyclophosphamide (Cytoxan, C). Side effects include vomiting, diarrhea, mouth sores, loss of hair, heart problems, low granulocytes, anemia, and low platelets. After six cycles over eighteen weeks, her hair, eyebrows and eyelashes fell out, but her immune system remained strong enough to complete the regimens. Her blood counts fell after each infusion, but recovered in time for the next assault. She kept her schedule.

We attended a Bears game at Soldiers Field in Chicago later that month, and the wind from Lake Michigan blew Laurene's wig off to the astonishment of the crowd around us. We attended the game with a Chicago lawyer and his wife. He was a business associate of mine. We had chosen not to broadcast Laurene's diagnosis outside of our family and close friends. Needless to say, Laurene's bald head surprised the couple. Fans below us passed the wig back up the aisles like a tray of nachos. Laurene laughed, and stuffed the wig into her coat pocket. After the game, we all went to lunch, and we brought them up to date.

Laurene was a modest person, and the wig incident had humiliated her. She didn't like exposing herself to anyone, and she dreaded any form of public humiliation. She had been raised around shy people, and people who were sensitive about their education, the kind of work they did, and how they looked. She told me how Neil never went beyond the eighth grade in school, but that he had practical intelligence. She said that even though Stella had graduated from college, she didn't have much self-confidence. You didn't put people down, or push them too far. You learned to overlook minor irritations and idiosyncrasies. In her business life, she would ignore chauvinistic comments, swearing, dirty jokes, and grouching. Everyone was entitled to a bad day, and besides, confronting people was not the way to get what you wanted.

When we were first married, Laurene told me never to criticize her in the presence of other people. "You can say whatever you want to me in private, but if you feel the need to criticize me in public, hold your tongue." The first time I made an open remark that Laurene deemed inappropriate, she tried to gently kick me under the table. I jumped a mile. She never tried that again. I have always been highly reactive to unexpected body contact; one reason I have never turned my cell phone on vibrate mode.

The accumulated effects of chemotherapy drugs left Laurene with nausea, constipation, and mouth sores. Her balance deteriorated to the point that when we walked together, I placed a hand under her elbow to keep her steady on her feet. Her skin felt tender and sensitive. She had difficulty sleeping. In the morning, I knew when she woke up, because she flapped her numb hands to restore circulation like a bird flapping its wings. She experienced the mental confusion and difficulty concentrating, which people call "chemo brain." Normally keeping everything in her head, she started to write things down on a calendar. Her periods gradually stopped with the early onset of menopause. "At least I'll never have hot flashes," Laurene said (she actually did).

The doctor kept telling Laurene how well she was doing compared to other patients. He encouraged her to take her pain medicine. He told her that addiction to drugs was rare in cancer pain management. She tried to keep a positive attitude. She ate healthy foods, and drank plenty of water. She tried to regard the harsh chemicals flooding through her body as agents of healing rather than poison. She kept up a mantra, *"breathe, think positive, you can do it."*

We flew back and forth from Grand Rapids for the infusions in Houston that were administered through a catheter inserted in Laurene's right forearm. We arrived early at the infusion therapy waiting room. The waiting room was smaller than most of the clinic waiting rooms, and sometimes there were no empty chairs, so patients sat in spare wheelchairs or on the floor. The wait time could range from one to six hours. Once a room opened, we might wait another hour for the drugs to arrive or for a special team to access the catheter. When the bags of drugs arrived, a nurse would read the names of the drugs and dosages to another nurse to make sure they were correct. The nurses also instructed us to keep a journal, but not the kind of journal we expected. They asked us to log in Laurene's reactions to the infusions—vomiting, nausea, diarrhea, hives, skin redness near the injection site—noting the date, time, intensity, and estimated volume of each occurrence.

Long hours would pass beneath the IV tree followed by more wait time after the infusions ended. The bright florescent lights glowered above us like a stationary sun on an endless day. There was no shade under the IV tree. The drip lines could not quench our thirst. No sound to soothe us other than the soft whirr of the infusion pump. I sat beside Laurene reading, or ran errands to check on future appointments, pick up prescriptions, bring back food from the cafeteria, or work through billing problems in the finance office (I received a two-inch stack of billing statements each month). The huge complex became so familiar to me, that even I couldn't lose my way.

Some days, I walked over ten miles through the corridors. I became adept at giving other people directions to remote areas in the clinic. After a while, I developed a sense that I belonged there, feeling good about having a place to be useful. I knew which way to turn after each stop on Elevator B.

One day, we arrived for an eleven o'clock morning appointment that ended at two the next morning. There had been a medical emergency with one of the patients, so the entire schedule backed up. Then, Laurene's medical file disappeared. I had to retrace her prior appointments over the last week, and finally found the large file in physical therapy. Over the next ten years, Laurene would go through this chemotherapy routine at least twenty-five times—low doses once a week, high doses every three weeks. After her veins deteriorated from the arm catheter, the doctors implanted a CVC (central venous catheter) in a large vein in her chest.

In April 1992, Laurene's blood counts had recovered sufficiently from the chemo to begin five weeks of pre-op radiation therapy to her chest. She stayed with her parents in Houston, and I went back to work in Grand Rapids, and took care of the children. I learned how to be a functional cook, but since I didn't get home from work until around seven, we went out to eat at places that Laurene would not have approved, like a sports bar where the girls and I played video trivia with biker dudes while gnawing on chicken wings and ribs, our fingers and hands bright orange from the hot sauce.

The girls seemed to be doing fine keeping up with their homework, and doing fun things with their friends. Meredith had been through Montessori school, and had learned to work independently. When I asked her if she needed help, she described her schedule of assignments, but only asked for help with one project. Odyssey of the Mind Project, an international creative problem solving program, drove me crazy. The project took weeks to complete, and when the contraption we invented neared completion, Meredith performed a test run. She donned her pink gymnastics tights and found a funny pink hat to wear on her head.

With a flourish of her baton, she set off a mousetrap screwed to a wooden plank. The energy from the sprung mousetrap spun two 33 speed vinyl records that I had found in the basement. The records were attached by an axle to a carved wooden car with a needle protruding from the front of the hood. Once in motion, the wheels moved towards the end of the plank where a large inflated pink balloon cowered. The needle popped the balloon while Meredith raised her head and arms to the sky in triumph like a magician who had pulled a rabbit out of her top hat. Relieved and surprised, I clapped, cheered, and hugged her. It wasn't rocket science, but it was science.

Our daughters knew that we loved them, and that they would not be abandoned no matter what happened to their mother. One evening, Meredith and I decided to take a selfie of the two of us wearing wire coat hangers under our chins and over the top of our heads with the hooks on top like antennae. We looked like a couple of silly space aliens. We had fun. During Laurene's absences, I took care of the girls, and the girls took care of me. Laurene had been the primary enforcer of the family rules. When she was in Houston, I had to be the bad guy once in a while. For example, one day a boy roared into our driveway on his new motorcycle. He wanted to take Jennifer for a ride. Helmet or no helmet, not on my watch, she had to stay put.

Laurene developed a happy routine of riding a bicycle each morning in her parents' neighborhood. Then she would drive down to the clinic for her radiation treatments. We talked everyday on the phone about details of her appointments, including profiles of her lab technicians and other people she met at the clinic. We talked about the challenges of her aging parents. I gave her daily reports on the children and their schedules. I talked about work. Haworth encouraged me to travel less, so I could be home with the girls, but managing on my own wasn't easy.

In addition to our activity reports, we discussed our ups and downs, our funny and scary dreams, and once in a while, our mutual fears that centered on side effects of the cancer— physical and mental side effects of the treatments, the emotional side effects on our relationship, the side effects on the kids and our parents. We worried that the cancer would overcome us in unforeseen ways causing our entire lives to become side effects of cancer. We constantly reassured each other that everything would be okay. Privately, we both worried about each other.

"Do you think you would benefit from some counseling?" Laurene asked.

"I don't think so, but maybe you should find a good therapist," I replied.

"I've never been to a shrink before. I'll have to do some research. I don't want a quack. Have you noticed all the signs for astrologers and palm readers we pass on Shepherd on the way to the clinic?"

"I wouldn't rule out anything. You never know, " I said. "Someday magicians might find a trick to cure cancer."

I waited in the car outside the counseling center. Laurene jumped in to report on her first therapy session. "He tried guided imagery on me." Her tone of voice gave me the impression that the therapist had assaulted her in some way, or pushed a big red button after attaching electrodes to her skull.

"He asked me to imagine my favorite color. When I told him that blue was my favorite color, he said that the color blue was too easy. He said to imagine purple. What kind of question is that? How will a crazy question like that help me? I'm a literal person. I can't do this."

"What did you expect?" I said.

"I thought psychologists listened, took notes...then told you what to do."

"Well, did he listen and take notes?"

"Yes, but he asked me to do things I can't do...ridiculous things. How would *you* describe purple?"

"Your eyes when you're angry, the sky at sundown, frosting on a birthday cake, the skin of an eggplant, the color of hope...."

"Sugar Bear, your mind and my mind are different."

"You need to see colors with your heart and mind."

"Easier for you than me."

When I asked her how the rest of the session went, she said that she had relaxed enough to fall asleep on the therapist's couch.

Laurene continued with the therapy for the next ten years. She not only learned to imagine the color purple, but after many sessions, she developed the ability to hypnotize herself. Self-hypnosis helped her manage extreme pain when morphine failed. Sometimes she took naps during her sessions, something she rarely did at home. Ever practical, if a therapy session was not working for her, at least the therapist had a good couch. When nothing helped, or she had a setback in her treatment, she used her favorite swear word, ***"RATS!"*** If she was really unhappy, she would add an addition rat or two, but I don't recall her ever using any other word. I never heard Neil swear, and certainly not Stella. Against the rules.

Talking with Laurene after her therapy sessions gave me insights into what Laurene most wanted from me as her husband. Laurene wanted my presence more than anything. She did not want me to be her therapist. She rarely shared her deepest emotions with me, partly because she didn't fully understand them herself. Her definition of emotional support was helping her to shower and dress, driving her to and from her appointments, taking notes during our clinic sessions, communicating with the outer circles of our friends and family so she could talk with the inner circle of her friends and family. So I had the impression that she preferred to do the housekeeping of her inner life, and she wanted me to do the yard work of her outer life. I had a difficult time understanding this for a long time, but it's what she wanted, not what I thought she wanted, that counted most.

Laurene divided her world into neat categories. Doctors followed scientific disciplines and objectivity, and psychologists indulged in subjective and untested theories of human behavior and mental processes. She walked through life with right and wrong, or good and bad categories most of the time like good and evil angels rested on her opposite shoulders. While she was highly intelligent, and could understand complexities and tones of gray in situations, she did not prefer middle categories or positions. Neil was like that.

For example, Laurene divided people and animals, including the girls and me, into either critters or varmints. When I asked her to explain the difference, she told me that critters were basically harmless creatures like squirrels and rabbits. They might get into mischief in your attic, but they were inherently cute and lovable like her daughters and me when we misbehaved. On the other hand, varmints were harmful like a coyote or a fox who would dig holes in the ground to break the legs of cattle, or steal chickens from the coop. Or like the poisonous snakes that lived in the muddy water tanks in Brownwood. When she didn't like our behavior, she called us varmints.

Laurene never referred to cancer as a journey. She never referred to cancer as a battle. The truth of the story of Laurene was tied to her odyssey to return to her life before cancer, to return home from Cancerland—the constant pressure to follow regimens, reverse setbacks, discount bad news, fight the pain, look for breaks—adapting, improvising, pretending, forgiving, and never wavering from her ambition to simply live.

For her, cancer was the Great Interrupter. It was not a mysterious force, a dramatic antagonist, or the voice of God. It certainly was not a blessing in disguise to test her faith or to make her a better person. Neither was cancer a payback for wrongdoing. She didn't want redemption. She wanted a cure. Her "adventure" was not coming home to God, but coming back to her house in Grand Rapids and her life before cancer. That's how it was.

Lennie was delighted. "That's it—that's it. Now tell how it is with us."

George went on. "With us it ain't like that. We got a future. We got somebody to talk to that gives a damn about us. We don't have to sit in no bar room blowin' in our jack jus' because we got no place else to go. If them other guys gets in jail they can rot for all anybody gives a damn. But not us."

Lennie broke in. "But not us! An' why? Because...because I got you to look after me, and you got me to look after you, and that's why."

Of Mice and Men by John Steinbeck

Randy Evans

Lesson Four

Suffering doesn't necessarily lead to redemption.

****

Novel (Excerpts)

Crooked River: Love and Adventure in Northern Michigan
(an excerpt from Red Sky Series, Book 3)

Prologue

"...have to stop your pay on Friday."

The personnel manager had said more, but the unexpected news shocked Rebecca Randall so much that she only registered part of his last sentence. She sat still and silent on the other side of his large desk with her hands folded in her lap. He peeked up from his paperwork, like a voyeur, to see her facial expression, thinking, *nothing more than a widening of the eyes. Most people have nothing to say, but you can tell a lot from their faces.*

Rebecca thought, *You bastard, you fired me! Better keep quiet. He's an idiot.* She lowered her head. He lowered his.

As the grandson of the company founder, Harrison Kindig had sifted down to the paperboard mill's lowest management position. Most of the time, he felt like an actor faking the playing of a musical instrument. People rarely asked him for advice. Most of the time, he sat alone in one of the few closed offices. He filled the time mumbling or thinking random thoughts. He hated to terminate office people, because he knew he might be next.

"Oh, I knew our days were numbered when the Clean Water Act passed...we had to stop making colored paperboard...so the dye decorated the Kalamazoo River with bright colors for a few days. Muskegon Orange was our best-selling shoebox board!"

He peered out of his floor-to-ceiling cubicle window at the long rows of gray desks occupied by accountants and schedulers, sitting at odd angles like gravestones in a cemetery. He glanced down at a globule of pancake syrup sticking to a liberty bell on the bicentennial tie he'd worn every Friday for nearly forty years. He wore short-sleeved shirts even in the winter. He had foregone long-sleeved shirts since the day a supervisor caught his long sleeve in the rotating blades of the pulp beater at the wet end of the board machine. By the time the poor man arrived at the dry end, he had become a sheet of paperboard. Only his belt buckle survived the city-block long machine. Harrison used the buckle to make a safety poster, until people complained, and began to call him an idiot.

Rebecca's dismissal at the mill had come out of the blue, abrupt—like sudden death. She fixed her eyes on Harrison's orange pocket protector bulging out from his dull-laundered shirt. Then came a scream—high and loud and long. The scream went on and on, until she unclenched her hands and clamped them over her mouth. She looked at the pear-shaped personnel manager in bewilderment. Where had the scream come from? How far had the sound traveled? Had the sound penetrated walls to the outer office? Had people heard the scream in the break room or the parking lot?

Harrison looked shivery white. He kept opening and closing his mouth, at a loss for words.

Finally, he said, "Okey Doke." He spilled coffee on his paperwork as he reached for the phone to call security.

When her mother had died, Rebecca hadn't screamed or even cried. When her brother died, she hadn't either. Not when her father had picked up and left town for good. But today she had screamed, as if losing her job had been a fate worse than an overload of death or fear of abandonment. An hour later after returning to her apartment, she still couldn't speak or move. Her routine had been altered. Her orderly and quiet life disrupted. Rebecca had worked at the paperboard mill since graduation from high school. What would she do next? She wondered.

Rebecca sat upright on a red vinyl kitchen chair, a remnant of her dead mother's kitchen. In the dull morning light, she faced the sooty factory window of her loft apartment. Her coffee pot gurgled on the counter. If anyone had been present, and had asked what seemed to be troubling her, she would have pulled at her long and straight brown hair, and said, "Oh, nothing."

For a decade, Rebecca had come home every morning from the night shift to eat breakfast at the diner across the street from her apartment, and then drop into a nest of pillows on her small bed, pet her cat and cuddle her stuffed bear. After four hours, she would rise and shower to work her day job at a nearby nursing home.

But this morning, Rebecca couldn't sleep. She edged her chair closer to the window. Her breath made small circles on the cold window panes. She felt stiff from sitting. When she had arrived from the mill into the cave-cold apartment an hour earlier, she had turned up the thermostat and sat down. Now she felt a bit dizzy. She needed air and light. Soot from the mill smokestack had silted her windowpanes like a gauzy veil. For the first time, she counted the panes in the old industrial window—sixteen grimy panes obscured by a hundred years of sloppy paint jobs on the grids.

Rebecca used both hands to raise the latch, and pushed open the hinged casement. The reluctant latch groaned. Pale morning light and a cold breeze filled the kitchen. She opened her eyes wider and took a deep breath. Spring would soon be here. Pigeon wings whirred above her. She ran a restless finger across the dust on the window sill, and watched dust balls fly away. She tried again to fathom the devastating news of the day. She knew others would take what happened as entirely common—*who hasn't lost a job?* Maybe she would have handled herself better if she had been given more notice, she didn't know.

Rebecca could only think in tiny thought fragments. Bits of nursery rhymes and pieces of her dead mother's admonitions drifted in and out of her mind as she sat back down on her kitchen chair. *Humpty Dumpty sat on a wall...think positive...all the king's horses and all the king's men couldn't put Humpty Dumpty together...had a great fall...take a deep breath...the itsy bitsy spider climbed up the water spout. She swallowed the bird to catch the spider that wiggled and jiggled and tickled inside her...honey, life isn't fair...nothing's for certain...down came the rain and washed the spider out. When you're older you'll be glad you have long legs. Most women dream of having long legs. Makes you look statuesque.*

If her mother had not died, she would have called her first. Her mother would have listened and told her that the layoff could not possibly be her fault. The two of them would have talked for an hour or so, and gotten off track onto other subjects, and those rambling sidetracks would have comforted Rebecca. Instead, she thought she might call her father. They rarely spoke. She had loved her father from a distance, and she believed that he loved her too in a way that she could not explain to herself or others. At this moment, she needed what she seldom required from others—

assurance and comfort. She had other family and a few friends, but no one really knew the inside of Rebecca. Today she had discovered something dark and uncontrollable about herself that scared her. Maybe she would talk things over with Mikage, her divorced friend, who owned the diner across the street.

It wasn't only the shock of losing her job that had kept Rebecca seated since returning to her apartment after the shift ended; it wasn't the accumulated weariness of working in the mill at night and sleeping during the day; and it wasn't the troubled solitary life she had led since losing her mother to cancer, her brother to a roadside bomb in Iraq, or the long absence of her father—it was her sudden outburst, something toxic within her that had leaked out and spread from the tiny personnel office to the shop floor, then out from the receiving dock onto the parking lot; surging to gush over the town and the round world— some *thing* more tangible than the sound of her scream, some *thing* not solid, but liquid and staining and of her own doing.

If she had been sitting in her apartment at the same moment of her termination, she might have heard her scream all the way from the mill. The long howl that seemed to Rebecca to have lasted as long as a tornado siren, or longer. A forever scream. She hated loud noises, especially unexpected ones.

Rebecca tried in vain to put things in perspective, but nothing worked. There was something very unpleasant about her unfathomable behavior in the personnel office. Where had her long, loud, piercing howl come from? What deep well inside her? Had she lost control of her emotions? For her, the insuppressible scream had exposed her in a way far worse than if she had thrown off her clothes and run through the office like a naked lunatic. She could not make the thoughts go away. The thoughts kept pulsing through her mind in stutter steps like irregular heartbeats.

O-M Gosh, why couldn't I have waited until I was outside in my car? I could've screamed my head off with the windows up, unnoticed. All these years, I've kept to myself. Never made a fuss. Now I'm gone from the face of their earth forever, and all they'll remember about me is the one day I lost it. I wish they had laid off someone else today and not me.

Rebecca and her stoic father had been the ones in the family to keep composed at her mother's memorial service five years earlier. Well-meaning people, who didn't even know her mother, openly wept while hugging her, and told her that she should have a good cry. Anne, her older sister, had called her for weeks afterwards to give her detailed accounts of her weekly grief therapy sessions. It seemed like everyone she knew told her to have a good cry, but Rebecca thought that if she ever started, she would not be able to stop, and besides, she failed to see the utility of emotional displays. *I can't stand people who get carried away at the least provocation. What good does it do?*

For months afterwards, her younger brother would say, "Becky—you sure you're all right? Do you want to talk about Mom?"

"Nah, I'm fine. Don't worry, okay?" Rebecca would say repeatedly. "I know Mom's up in heaven and still loves me." She didn't believe her own words, but she had to say something.

Rebecca had wanted to comfort Michael like her mother had always comforted her. She wanted to say: *I don't know how to live without Mom, and I don't know what's going to happen to us without her. I love you, Mikey!* But Rebecca was more like her father—serious and self-contained. Her mother had said she had been quiet as a child. As an adult, she was still awkward and formal with other people, a creature of habit, and cautious about taking risks—like an old lady living inside the body of a young woman. Now, the slow, creaky wheel of her world was about to turn.

Rebecca lived in a small town north of Kalamazoo. She rented in a former carriage factory built like a fortress in the 1800s. Her unit sat on the top floor, marked by a single floor-to-ceiling window. Brick, timber, and concrete surrounded her. She wondered how many workers over how many years had looked out the same fourth-story window longing to be outside.

In her case, she didn't long to be outside. She felt safe inside. For her, the apartment was a place of solid certainty, a place where she knew her neighbors, knew familiar sounds in the stairways and hallways, and the sounds above and below her. She knew how her key turned the bolts in the door locks. Her life had been predictable and reliable, within prescribed upper and lower limits of acceptability, like the quality control charts that she had meticulously maintained at the mill. And living in solitary, she had no need to explain why at her age she slept with a cat and a stuffed bear tucked to her breast at night.

Looking out over the town through the open window focused her eyes. In the town, Rebecca could walk most everywhere she needed to go. She leaned forward and observed how the haphazard, wide curves of the dark black river broke up the neat street grid like someone had run a grease pen over the rows and columns of a spreadsheet. The careless curves of the river reminded her of the scar the surgeon had left on her mother's chest. At the time, she had hated the surgeon for making her mother's body less than perfect—cutting away the soft, abundant bosom that had provided boundless comfort to her throughout her childhood.

A few years earlier, a flash flood had raised the dark river waters beyond the banks, and covered some of the lower streets. Rebecca had to improvise her usual walking route to work. It was a minor inconvenience for her, but some homes had been swept away in torrents of rainwater. At the time, Rebecca had thought how lucky she was to live on the top floor of the solid old building, safe and secure behind her solid door.

Rebecca looked out on the shabby street as if for the first time: time-worn buildings with cracked and water-stained walls that were secured both day and night, former shops with rotted plywood boarding up the windows, and soon-to-be-out-of-business bars and restaurants with tired-looking chairs and stained table tops, where people's who had lived here when times were better sat and looked out on the pot-hole-filled street lined with battered, broken down cars with their tires gone, and deserted broken sidewalks strewn with weeds. Signs advertised businesses that no longer existed, and weathered "under repair" signs bent over like beaten-down people who somehow managed to keep standing. Delivery trucks coughed down the street on their way to more prosperous parts of town.

She sat back down on the kitchen chair, and continued to face the outside. Morning shadows were beginning to break away from her side of the street. A mother hustled her children along the sidewalk prompting thoughts of times past. She angled sideways to see the family snapshots taped to the refrigerator door.

Rebecca decided to call a few people who had worked with her to let them know what had happened.

She had assumed that she would grow old working down by the river—a quiet, sensible way to live. She had started at the mill right after high school. She had thought about college, but her mother's long illness had taken a bad turn, and it was more sensible to be the one child who stayed home. She didn't mind. She had never thought twice about it. She had been a mature child. Someone had to take care of her mother, and her father.

A train whistle blew near the crossing on Main Street. *A signal controlled by a pull cord. A low-pitched short blast with a purpose. Not a horror-movie scream like mine. I'm such an idiot! Why can't I stop thinking about this!*

Rebecca pulled the hairpins and elastic out of her long brown hair, and let strands fall across her pale face and down her white sweater. The tallest girl in her high school class at five foot ten, Rebecca had played basketball all the way to state regionals in her junior year. After her mother's illness progressed in her senior year, Rebecca cared for her after school and on weekends at home, and later, at the nursing home. She had always managed a date for important occasions like proms and holiday dances. Since high school, she had dated one boy after another, but no one she really liked. *I should have spent more time finding a serious boyfriend. Not so easy working nights. But there's no one to hold me here now that my job's gone. My work was my life in this town.*

One day two mill hands had observed her leaving the lunch room:

"There goes that Randall girl, the basketball player. She's tall and thin like a heron, but not bad looking. My son asked her out, but she turned him down flat, who knows why? If you ask me, she's odd like her father—hard to know, a bit stuck up if you ask me."

"She smiled at me once when we passed in the parking lot," the other mill hand said. "A nice smile, but off a step—you know, like she had to think first."

After the loss of his wife and son, Nick Randall had left town looking for solitude. Rebecca understood why her father had left to live in northern Michigan, and tried not to feel abandoned. *Bury the past and start over. That's what he's doing. Vietnam had changed him forever from how I remembered him as a little girl. He never talked about it, but his silence spoke more than words. Maybe losing Mom and Michael had pushed him over the edge. He had to leave. He wouldn't have left me if he felt he had a choice. He had to find another place to suffer alone. I couldn't comfort him. Only Mom could do that. Only Mom could comfort me. So I get it.*

Rebecca thought she might visit her father Up North, or her sister who lived on a ranch in Montana. She decided to visit her father first. He lived much closer. A few miles inland from Lake Michigan, his cottage sat on a riverbank called Devil's Elbow, a sharp bend in the Crooked River. She took another look at the photo of her family. *It seems a long time since we lived together.* She looked how her arms were draped over her Dad's shoulders in the snapshot. *All arms and legs then. I'm the same now. I want to see my Dad. Maybe I can be a hermit like him.*

Chapter One
The Mill Personnel Office

Rebecca replayed the scene of her demise one more time.

Harrison Kindig had found Rebecca by the time clock, and asked her to come to his wood-paneled office behind the reception desk. On her way to his office, Rebecca stopped by her locker to pull out a white sweater to cover her denim work shirt. She washed her hands and face in the locker room sink, and pinned her hair to one side. She arrived at his half-open door, and he beckoned her in with his pudgy forefinger. He carried his large round belly on short legs with short arms. He settled into his chair like wet cement.

Rebecca sat down on a metal folding chair closest to the door, straight-backed with her long arms dropped and her hands folded in her lap. She leaned forward and looked up at the personnel manager across his polished oak desk which was raised above the floor. His back faced the window, so on a sunny day if you looked up at him from the other side of his desk, you had to squint to see him. Rebecca never ran into him much at the mill, because he stayed in his office and she never got in trouble. She noticed his baldish head. *When he interviewed me ten years ago, he had hair.* A large wart on his cheek looked like a third eye. Rebecca tensed her body as if she was about to be punched in the stomach. Not much good ever happened in this office.

"Would you mind shutting the blinds?" Rebecca said. The window glare on the vast polished desk hurt her eyes. Her hands clenched.

"Oh, not at all." Harrison swiveled slowly and mechanically towards his one window, careful not to slide the high-backed chair off the platform that he had constructed from a discarded wooden pallet he found in the mill. (He wanted to look down on all the people who sat before him, but he was short, and he was angry because of his shortness, so he was angry all the time.) He tugged on the blind cord until the slats closed half way, a compromise to demonstrate that he was the one in charge who pulled the strings.

Rebecca looked down to see narrow black prison stripes of blocked sunlight fall through the window and cross her white sweater, giving it the appearance of a prison jumper. Harrison sank back into his chair, and gripped chair arms tightly like he was ready for takeoff on a rocket ship. His red face beaded with sweat like he had been doing honest labor. He removed his suit coat ceremoniously, and draped it over the chair back. He stared down on her, and then he cranked open his mouth slowly like his jaw operated by hoist from an internal crane, or from the deft hand movements of an invisible puppeteer above him. Then, he hesitated like he was about to mouth a name he'd forgotten.

"Uh, Rebecca—we all like you—Rebecca. But we have to lay you off. Now you can come around here any time you want…but we have to stop your pay on Friday." His voice sounded tired, stiff, and breathless to Rebecca, her name sounded like it had been inserted into a fill-in-the-blank sentence.

For a moment, Rebecca sat motionless and mute. She wanted to say something, but her throat tightened, and she felt weak in her arms and legs. She tried to focus on the orange pocket protector bulging out of Harrison's shirt pocket. She raised her eyes to his butterfat neck, and then to his dilated eyes. Harrison ran his fingers tenderly over his scalp, as if searching for his lost hair. Then he yawned while looking down at the paperwork through his drugstore bifocals, removed a motel pen from his orange pocket protector, and tapped the pen on the paperwork. *"Tap...tap...tap."* The tapping sounded to Rebecca like a jackhammer.

"***Friday?***" The word before her uncontrollable scream. The moment before the breach point of a flood-swollen river. After calling security, Harrison backed his chair off the riser. He toppled over, and rolled on the floor like a tortoise.

***

Now still sitting still in her kitchen, she tried to take deep breaths and forget. She knew a bigger world lay out there somewhere beyond her small life centered on work at the mill. The town's streets, the train tracks, and the river came and went from somewhere. *My world will no longer run on its old, safe tracks. My job was safe—then gone. I've been cut loose! What do you do when your life keeps going on and going on like a river, then one day doesn't?*

Outside her window, she heard birdsongs warbling everywhere, so many species interrupting each other talking of the cold spring. The sounds overwhelmed her. She placed her hands over her ears and closed her eyes, trying to shut out the unwanted flood of light and sound. Shut down what had happened. As she took another deep breath, she inhaled the pleasant aromas from Mikage's diner. She could almost taste the bacon smoke. Her hunger pangs returned, reminding her that she hadn't eaten since the mid-shift break at three.

She stood up and walked over to her cupboard, and pulled out a bag of stale Oreos. A black ant skittered behind a box of oatmeal. For the first time in years, she noticed her broken toaster on the counter, and thought about how she had kept all the equipment in her quality control lab operating in perfect condition, each one labeled with a service date. She returned to her chair and looked out the window again while she took a test bite of an Oreo, then tossed the bag into the waste basket under her sink.

Rebecca lived on this backstreet a few streets off Main, a fifteen-minute walk from the mill. She was twenty-eight. Her florescent-white face provided a canvas for her wide, almond-shaped hazel eyes. Above her eyes rose a furrowed brow beyond her age. She was slender from walking nights from one end of the mill to the other (filling sample orders, performing process checks, designing quality experiments, updating control charts, going back and forth across the sprawling mill). She ran her hands through her long, dark brown hair. Her hair felt damp, stringy, unkempt. Maybe she would draw a bath in her claw-foot tub, wash her hair and feel less upset. She unlaced her heavy shoes, and placed them by the door where they belonged. A place for everything, and everything in it's place.

The third shift had ended at seven. *I was employed, but now I'm not.* More than an hour after dismissal, she continued sitting in the kitchen chair, looking out the window over her familiar universe—unshaken by her personal earthquake, carrying on as if nothing had happened. She knew that she should do something, maybe take off her stinky work clothes and bathe. However, she remained stunned, staring down on the sparse street activity one moment, into the orange and pink morning sky the next, and then out through the smoky window panes to a vitiated view of the river, no longer the blue ribbon in her mind's eye, but a gray and swollen thread. She felt zombie-like, like the view of her world had been altered by what had happened.

After a long time, Rebecca looked back again into the interior of the apartment. Her mother's empty flower vase sat on the floor in a corner. Her mother had gathered wild flowers for the vase in the warm months *to have beauty in the house.* **Beep, beep, beep**, the coffee maker timer took her once again back to the counter. The unexpected sound set off the same sudden swelling-balloon feeling she had experienced in the personnel office when she had been discharged. She felt like she was going to explode inside. She yanked the useless toaster cord out of the outlet, smashed the toaster against the enamel of the stove, and threw it into the waste basket on top of the bag of Oreos. *I'm out of control*—she thinks. *Why did I do that?*

Rebecca had forgotten about the coffee. She poured the steamy coffee into a white ceramic mug. Holding the mug in two shaky hands, she returned to the chair to sit near the window again. She began to perspire through her blue work shirt from the warmth of the rising sun filtering through the windows and from the steam rising from her coffee cup.

Scratchy, her tortoiseshell tabby cat, shuffled in from the bedroom, and nuzzled the back of Rebecca's legs. The cat moved with the languor of a bored queen moving through the inner rooms of an ancient palace. The sudden noise in the kitchen had woken her from morning slumbers. Scratchy didn't have a clue as to what had happened with Rebecca at the end of the shift. The cat was as indifferent as the occasional people passing below her on the sidewalk.

Rebecca's eyes followed the colorless dead leaves scattering on the red street bricks below, leftovers from the previous autumn—bleached little skeletons. It rained hard the night before, and a Styrofoam cup bobbled in a muddy puddle that had formed over one of the tire-busting potholes.

She would miss some of the old-timers, all of the petty confidences and life dramas of her co-workers, and the old instruments and gauges in the quality control lab where she worked. She would also miss the predictability of the third shift, and its comfortable routine. Everything was familiar: the parking lot, the locker room, the break room, the machine rooms, the maintenance and tool shops, the inspection and testing labs, the shipping and receiving docks, and the warehouse. Now all she had left was her part-time job at the nursing home a few blocks away. It didn't pay much, but had been enough to supplement her pay at the mill. Like the mill, her work there was predictable; even emergencies were routine.

Of all the mill people, she would most miss David, the security guard.

Chapter Two
The Security Guard

The personnel manager called David. David and Rebecca had dated for a short time, and several years ago, had come close to having sex behind stacked skids of paperboard in a dark corner of the finished goods department. It was a remote part of the mill where people seldom traveled except by forklift to drop off or pick up loads on pallets or skids. The skids were stacked two high in long rows, each marked with a tag indicating the customer, grade, and weight. It was a cold winter Saturday morning, and they had run into each other, each holding a clipboard to tally the inventory. Their breath steamed while they talked. The encounter was not accidental.

"I volunteered for this, but they didn't tell me how to fill out these forms," David said. He knew Rebecca would help him, because she seemed to know how to do everything around the mill, but he had wanted an excuse to see her and had been looking for her all morning. David had recently completed a combat tour in Afghanistan, and lived at home with his parents while he went to school. His dark blue uniform outlined a muscular, trim soldier's body. David and Rebecca had been attracted to each other since the first day they had met, but they kept each other at arm's length, submitting to the rules of working in the same place. And they were both shy people.

But when they moved their heads together to examine a spreadsheet on her clipboard, the proximity was too much for them. His bristled beard touched her hair as it hung down over the clip board, and then he moved closer, clacking the frames of his safety glasses against hers. Hidden in the dim light of the warehouse, he removed his glasses and then hers. David gave her a benign kiss, and Rebecca kissed him back hard. They kissed and pressed against each other until David's security badge arrested them by pricking Rebecca's breast.

"We're breaking the rules," Rebecca said. Every year for ten years, Rebecca had reviewed the employee personnel manual to avoid any infractions. Each year, she looked at revisions for new rules."

"Rebecca, you're the only one I know who'd think about the employee handbook at a time like this!"

"I've always thought it best to follow the rules—" she said. She ran her hands over his chest. Intense desire welled up from the same dark place in her body that had more recently generated her scream. She struggled to keep herself under control. She retreated to the safety of her more reliable mind.

"I've got condoms," David said.

"Where?"

"In my wallet."

"With your cash and credit cards?"

"Yep."

"How many?"

"I don't know...maybe four."

"Four?"

"Yeah, you know, in case one gets ripped or torn."

"Have you checked the expiration dates?"

"No. I picked up a carton at the PX in Afghanistan."

"A carton? How long ago was that? What were you doing buying cartons of condoms in Afghanistan?"

"Yeah, well, we used them to cover the muzzles of our rifles. Best thing to keep the sand out."

"So you want to use an old condom on me, and nine months later I have a baby security guard?"

"Well...?" David said. His blue eyes penetrated Rebecca. She let go. She had temporarily lost her mind.

Looking sideways to make sure they were alone, they unlaced and removed their safety shoes, work pants and shirts, trying not to look at each other, as if they were about to take a quick shower in the locker room. Neither one could manage to remove their underwear. Then David looked down at her legs, and nudged Rebecca's back up against a skid piled with sheets of paperboard, still warm from running through the laminator. His eyes looked wild. The metal skid straps dug into Rebecca's back. Pain broke the spell like the security badge had done before.

She pushed David back, *"Can't!"* she said. "Sorry, no, I'm not ready. No way, no way in hell—not in the mill with a guy who walks around with condoms in his wallet. And we could both lose our jobs. You're supposed to protect me from people like you."

Strong feelings ran through her mind and body in all directions: passion, pain, guilt, shame, fear, embarrassment, and a touch of humor. But she managed to pull herself together, and spoke in a low voice as they put their clothes back on.

"Well, that was very nice and sudden," she said. "I've always had a thing for you, David, but I've never let you know. I don't flirt...one of my failings, I guess." David's face glowed red, his neck veins bulged blue, and he breathed hard.

"Lord, Lord, Rebecca. I'm not a flirt either. I apologize for getting so ...best if we don't say a thing about this for now...not that we *did* anything."

They both stood in the vast, cold, dim space of the mill to catch their breath. Then Rebecca looked straight into his eyes. She no longer felt panicked.

"Kiss me like a friend," she said.

"All righty." David hugged her, and kissed her cheek.

"Do you still need help with the forms?" Rebecca asked.

"Nope, that was just an excuse to see you."

"*You!*"

"Sorry. But I don't feel apologetic about seeing those long legs of yours. I've never seen legs like that. I'll keep thinking about those legs for a long time."

"So that's the best you've got for compliments? My legs? Well, go on now," she smiled and pushed her hands against his chest. He disappeared into the warehouse mist. *When are you going to figure out how to be around men? Guess my Mom was right. Long legs have advantages.*

***

The encounter embarrassed them both. They avoided each other for weeks, and then went out on a few dates. They decided to be friends, but the memory of their encounter lingered in the background of their polite daily exchanges.

David had taken her back to the lab where she packed a small box of personal items (she gave him a popular book on leadership), and then he walked her out to her car and gave her a hug. Rebecca said, "I have nothin' after ten years. Nothin'."

"Rebecca, I'm sorry that you have to go," David said.

"I'm sorry I have to go, too."

"Stay in touch. Even though we didn't work out, you gave me hope, you know, hope about—"

"Yep, I'll stay in touch," she interjected. "Let me know when you finish school. I'll come to your graduation."

"O.K., but that'll be sometime."

"Whenever. I'll come. I guess you know I'm dependable."

"Rebecca, I can tell you're down."

"A little. I feel like my life's fallen out from under me like a trap door."

"When I get down, I fish my way out of it."

"Fish?"

"Yes, there's nothing like fishing for when you feel bad."

"I haven't fished since I was little. Maybe I will, or maybe I'll find something *like* fishing," she smiled.

"What else is *like* fishing?" he said.

"Well, I don't know, but if I find out, I'll let you know."

"Yep, if you find something *like* fishing, let me know," David said. "Might save me a whole lot of time. Oh, and can I tell you something else?"

"What?"

"It's about that scream of yours."

"Oh, that. I'm so sorry."

"No, I liked your scream. Never heard a scream like that. I thought it was a fine scream. *Everybody* said so."

"So *everybody* heard it?"

"Yep, I heard you out here in the parking lot. And even though I never heard you scream before, I knew the scream was yours. It sounded like a horror movie scream. I thought you had died in that scream before you reached the middle. What I want to say about your scream—you've got to have something valuable behind a scream like that—talent of some sort. I mean, that was a four-part harmony scream, like all the soprano ladies in the church choir let go at once."

"I'll keep that in mind. Maybe I could find a job where you have to scream a lot." She gave him a hug.

"You could get good pay for a scream like that," he said. "Have you ever thought about the power of the human screaming voice?"

"David, sometimes I think of you for a few minutes before I fall asleep at night." Rebecca placed her hand on his shoulder. "You're a kind man, and I want you to be happy."

"Well, I used to whistle before I went overseas to combat, and now I'm whistling again because of you. It's not much, but—"

"Whistling's good," Rebecca said. "Whistling beats screaming any day of the week."

***

Rebecca returned her awareness to the present once again. The sixteen panes in the window reflected the light in a different way, capturing a separate slurry of sky and clouds. Each pane seemed to frame a separate country with its own sky and clouds. She reached out and raised the casement higher until the glass reflected the busted up pieces of concrete and tall weeds that were once a sidewalk.

What would it be like to live without her work? How would she feel each new hour of each new day? She would no longer have to try to stay awake in the scheduling meetings, pretend to be interested in maintenance routines, keep the control charts updated or the sample requests filled. No more night shift. What would it be like to sleep through the night, and wake refreshed in the morning?

Then out of nowhere, she said out loud, "I feel like an awful leftover." She thought about her mother and brother and father, but especially her mother. She had always reported her personal triumphs and disasters to her. Since her mother had died, she had lost any sense of having a future. Who would she tell her dreams to? The mill had been more a kind of limbo than a path to somewhere. For another moment she stood stone still, then ran her finger across the window frame and watched dust balls float away.

As she turned away from the window, Rebecca remembered how her father used to lean his head towards her as if speaking in confidence, and in his gruff, husky voice would say, "Becky, you're the one in the family with both feet on the ground." She never knew what he meant exactly, only that he was happy she had graduated from high school, stayed out of trouble, and held a steady job.

Steadfast, she offered the rest of the family a framework of easy-going responsibility. Her quiet presence provided a stable architectural element to their family life, like an open window through which a steady breeze flowed. What would her father think now? She walked from the kitchen into the bedroom and began to undress. She looked down on the folds and hollows of her body. She felt she might cry. Then her tornado of emotions came to rest for the moment. She wanted a bath. She wanted her cat. She wanted her stuffed bear.

Chapter Three
Mikage's Diner

Rebecca folded her work clothes, then set out fresh clothes for her afternoon job. Her bed was still made from the day before. She didn't want to sleep. She wanted to stay up all day, and go to bed at night like other people did.

She drew her bath water, and slipped into the tub, letting the warm water surround her exhausted body and soak her long, brown hair with a filmy, soft membrane. She splayed out her spindly legs, and rested her long, narrow feet on the edge of the tub. She thought about how she had long-neglected her feet—they were calloused and most of her toenails were broken. She slipped them back under the water, and closed her eyes.

When her eyes opened again, she realized that she had nodded off. The bath water was cold and still, and reflected the bare light bulb on the ceiling. The sky had changed to a threat of rain. Her body felt liquefied.

Dressed in a clean shirt and jeans, Rebecca dropped down the narrow wooden staircase to the street, and walked across to the diner, where she looked forward to her daily breakfast of *huevos rancheros* and coffee. The place had emptied the usual breakfast crowd, so Mikage was alone. Bacon and coffee smells lingered in the air.

The diner was a small operation, with a long counter, eight booths, and a tiny but efficient kitchen. The walls were painted pink with little adornment; the interior well-lighted, a sharp contrast to the drab colors on the street. A radio played seventies music on low volume. Mikage Hoshimoto was behind the counter, elbow-deep in dish suds. Unlike Rebecca, Mikage could never stop moving. When she talked, she never stopped working. The two women seldom said "hello" or "good-bye," as if their relationship was just one continuous conversation.

Mikage was a tiny, but strong, woman nearing seventy. Her thick hair was short, grayish black, and covered with a lime-green bandana. Her skin was lemony and smooth. She talked quickly, with her dark eyes flashing with each word. Rebecca marveled at her fluid, ballet-like movements through the kitchen and dining area, all the while talking either to others or to herself. She often talked to her customers in their native tongues, shifting easily from one language to another. Rebecca could only make out Spanish, but Mikage spoke many more languages. Rebecca admired her physical and mental fluency.

"Why so late?" Mikage said.

"I lost my job."

"So you don't—"

"No."

"But what—"

"I don't want to talk about it now."

"If you don't talk, how will I know what happened?"

"Please, not now."

Mikage wiped her hands, then poured orange juice and coffee for Rebecca. Then Rebecca gave her usual order, and Mikage began preparing breakfast. She cracked two eggs on the grill with one hand, and turned over some corn tortillas steaming on the back of the grill. Rebecca could smell garlic, cilantro, jalapeño, cumin, onions, and tomatoes.

Then Mikage gave Rebecca her usual rapid-fire update on the neighborhood news including where the homeless man was sleeping, details of the high school trash pickup project, the yoga instructor's latest trip to India, and recent foreclosures. Regarding personal matters, the women were rarely open with each other, but more open than with anyone else. The common ground between the two resided in a keen interest in the goings on in their mutual territory: new people moving in and out of the block, real estate transactions, arrests, arguments, lost dogs and cats, large and small eyesores, unusual street people, doors left ajar and broken windows. She kept moving to and from the grill until her masterpiece was ready. She sprinkled fresh cilantro and crumbles of feta cheese over the top.

"So you don't want to talk about losing your job?"

"Okay, the mill laid me off today...said it was permanent."

"They'll call you back."

"No they won't."

"You made too much money," Mikage said.

"What do you mean?"

"When you do good work, you get raises. But then your pay gets high, and they think they can find someone cheaper to do the job, so they get rid of you."

"That's not what happened."

"Yes, that's what happened."

"No."

"Oh, I know you. You think you did something wrong."

"No."

"Yes, you blame yourself."

"No."

"Well you didn't."

"Didn't what?"

"Do something wrong."

"I know."

"So get busy and find another job."

"It's not that easy."

"Yes, it is. Here's the paper. Start looking."

Mikage said all this in about seven seconds while she moved around the counter and grabbed a discarded newspaper from one of the empty booths.

"There isn't anything else for me here...the work's gone away," said Rebecca. "I might move."

"You better not."

"When they told me, I screamed."

"Good for you."

"I screamed my head off."

"Good for you!"

"I had kept my cool for all these years—"

"I love to scream. I don't even need a reason."

"I felt embarrassed."

"So that's why you want to leave town? Because you screamed?"

"That's one reason."

"If you leave, I will follow you like a stray dog." Her plain round face was swollen with tears.

"I have no idea where to go." Rebecca felt tears of her own.

"This town is shrinking. Too small for us."

"It was a living."

"I will sell the diner."

"For now, I want to visit my father."

"No jobs where he lives. So why visit?"

"I want to see him. He's my family."

"No, he's your father. *I'm your family.*"

"Yes, you are."

"My parents are dead," said Mikage. She reached into a refrigerator for a jar of pickled ginger. "Can you believe people like sushi in this little town?"

"You're a good cook."

"I made breakfast for you on your first day of work."

"I remember."

"Rebecca, please don't leave me here alone." She wiped her face with a tea towel.

"I'll visit my father, and figure out what to do next," Rebecca shrugged.

"A man with a job would help us both. But no one wants an old Japanese woman."

"I don't think anyone wants me either," Rebecca replied.

"I don't know why. I think you're perfect."

"Perfect?"

"Yes, perfect," said Mikage.

"I liked David at the mill, but he was too nice. Nice doesn't work for me. It's not enough."

"I had a husband who was *not* nice. Nice is good. Nice men treat you good, and you can boss them around," said Mikage.

"I'm not the bossy type."

"You know what you need? You need to throw a fit."

"I did. I smashed my toaster."

"Bring me the toaster. I'll make it good as new. Now you must go sleep."

An old man walked in the door with a smile for Mikage and his daily weather report: "It's sunny this morning, but rain's on the way!" Mikage walked over to the booth where he parked his walker and edged into the seat. None of his clothes matched. He was looking for an early lunch and his daily dose of kindness from Mikage.

"See ya later, alligator. If you're not too tired after the nursing home, come over for supper. I'll fix you something special."

"After while crocodile." Rebecca walked back across the street rubbing the creases in her forehead.

A dog had flopped down on bricks in the middle of the street to take a nap, and Rebecca stopped to talk him over to the sidewalk. From an open upper story window, faint oldies music played from a crackling radio. After she climbed the narrow stairway to her apartment, she grabbed her stuffed bear, and dropped into bed with her clothes on. She would have to get back up in a few hours, but for now she needed sleep.

Chapter Four
The Memory Unit

Rebecca woke from her nap, and changed clothes. Most days she walked to the nursing home. The walk helped her wake up.

Rebecca looked down from her window. Low, steel-gray clouds were drifting in from the Northwest and spitting rain. People detoured around the dog still sleeping on the sidewalk as they headed for cover. She drove several blocks to the edge of town, and pulled in at the back of the parking lot, away from the visitor parking. Dodging fat raindrops, she ran to the door in the dull afternoon light.

Inside the one-story brick buildings, she walked down a series of familiar hallways and pressed the large red security button that opened the double doors to the memory unit. In the dining room, Tom and Calvin sat tethered to their wheelchairs. Large white bibs covered their plaid shirts. Calvin talked to Tom as if they were having a conversation. Calvin's words ran together in soft, disconnected murmurs.

His uninflected tones soothed Rebecca. In fact, the whole ambiance of the memory unit was a soothing space for her. Here there was no fear of disaster, because disaster had already struck. And the memory of disaster had been erased in favor of an eternally new world revolving around the moment. The retired businessmen sat facing each other across a table. Cal had quit talking months before, but Tom went on as usual.

"Too many meetings, Cal," Tom said, "Too many meetings around here." Cal responded with a rigid smile.

When Rebecca approached the table, Tom turned in her direction as if his neck had been fused to his torso. "Where's my departure gate? I have the three o'clock to Chicago."

Rebecca lowered her face so that it was even with his and ran her hand through his white halo of hair. She said with a sweet smile, "No more flights today."

"Well, okay then," he said. He turned to silent Cal, "Looks like I'm going to miss a board meeting." Cal still smiled like a gentle piece of carved granite. Through the cafeteria window, the dark clouds were drawing closer, and the wind shook the chain-linked fence bordering the nursing home.

Tom looked out at the sky beyond the fence, and reached for Rebecca's hand. He whispered, "Watch out for subs!"

These bizarre exchanges happened all the time, but Rebecca respected what they represented—thin lines that connected dementia patients to their pasts;

sometimes stirring faint hope and desire. A few days earlier, the social worker had stopped Rebecca in the hallway, and mentioned that Tom had offered her money to spring him loose. Rebecca replied, "He wants his old world back—his house, his lawn, his wife, his dog. That's what he wants."

Rebecca completed her usual chores, and then helped with the afternoon fill-in-the-blank word games and balloon volleyball. At the end of her shift, blowy sheets of rain flooded the parking lot, so she decided to take a different exit than usual. She entered a long windowless series of attached parking garages that would take her closer to her car without going outside. The security lights glowed orange through the dark cement-surfaced building interiors. She made her way past old cars, discarded sofas, old TV's and stereos, mildewed shower curtains, dark green plastic bags filled with discarded clothes, and a rusted-out snow blower—remnants of what she imagined to be dead people's stuff. *So this was what remained after the bodies were shipped to the embalmers and cremators—a mess for the janitor.*

While she walked, she thought that the deluge must have triggered Tom's warning to look out for submarines. He once told her how he had commanded a Sub Chaser in World War II. He had probably navigated his boat through storms like this. Perhaps the chain-linked fencing outside the nursing home had reminded him of a ship's railing, and the vortex of his diseased mind blew him back to stormy seas and hidden dangers under the water. Submarines—part of his shrinking inventory of memories.

At the far end of the garage space, Rebecca came across a ten-foot high pile of discarded aluminum walkers. The walkers were thrown together at different angles. The sum of their awkward shapes smoothed to the symmetry of a bell. Dumbstruck, she crouched down and stared at the aluminum mountain. In the weak, orangish light of the parking garage, the pile of walkers looked like a fire-lit assemblage of white bones from some ancient altar. More remnants of old people's stuff.

Rebecca felt sad and cried for the cruelty, confusion, and general misery of people who suffer in the world. She felt powerless to help fenced-in Tom and frozen-jawed Cal. What would become of Tom's home, his dog, his car, and the lawn he had cared for?

Like Tom, she was looking for a departure gate. She felt like the jumbled heap of walkers—a leftover from a world that no longer existed. Then she cried for herself. She bent over for a time like a folded-up lawn chair and wept for a long time. When she finished, she sat upright with her legs crossed, and rocked back and forth to the rhythm of the rain drumming on the sheet metal roof. After wiping her eyes and blowing her nose, she unfolded herself and walked out of the parking garage into the rainstorm. Little pellets of hail scattered across the asphalt like broken strings of pearls. She didn't know why, but she felt better.

***

Rebecca dropped into her car, drove back to her apartment, and changed into dry clothes. She laughed when she looked at her growing pile of laundry, and thought how many times she had changed clothes since leaving the mill that same morning that now seemed so long ago. She had left the window open so the inside of the apartment felt like the outside. A puddle of rainwater sat on the floor below the window. A large black fly announced its buzzy presence on the sill. Rebecca latched the window, and walked over to Mikage's. A "closed" sign hung from the locked door, because Mikage served only lunch and dinner. Mikage saw her coming. It was after six.

When Mikage opened the door, Rebecca smelled the fragrances of miso ramen soup coming from the steamy kitchen: fish stock, cilantro, spinach, green onions, snow peas, corn, bamboo shoots, tofu, snow peas, pork, mushrooms, fish cakes, and bean sprouts. Mikage poured hot sake into cups from a large carafe. For the next hour, the two women chose not to talk about the future, but simply enjoyed each other's company. At the last possible moment when Rebecca was half way out the diner door, Mikage gave her a side hug. "Poor kid. Are you okay?"

"Yep. I was tired and hungry when I came in this evening, but I feel fine now. I'm going to put on my nightshirt and relax before I go to bed."

"I'm happy you feel better," Mikage said. "I know you might leave...I understand. Good night, my perfect friend."

***

Rebecca crossed the black street. The single street light on the block was out. No moon. No stars. She bent over and looked down at the uneven bricks in order to keep her footing. She was a bit tipsy from the sake. What had become of the sleeping dog? If someone had been looking out a window at her crossing the street, they would have described the figure of an old woman. As she entered the old building, her mother's words echoed against the hard surfaces all around her: *Life's not fair. Life's not fair.* She fed her cat, slipped into her nightshirt and slippers, but wasn't ready for bed.

For the next few hours, Rebecca engaged in her one hobby. Rebecca made paper out of recycled clothing. She liked her work: making something new out of rags, crafting paper using methods hundreds or even thousands of years old, using methods first employed by paper mills in Spain and the parchment makers of ancient Egypt. She produced high quality archival paper. The satisfaction of making paper helped to calm her in the wake of losing her job. It was a meditative activity—stirring the fibers with a wooden rake to disperse them evenly, forming a sheet of paper on her rectangular wooden frame, peeling off the large damp handkerchief of paper from a corner of the frame, clamping it in a screw press to dry overnight. Her own little paper factory where no one could lay her off.

Now beyond tired, Rebecca shuffled from her small corner workshop to bed. In the short interval before sleep took over, she tried to imagine herself in a new life, but failed to think of herself in any other way.

Chapter Five
Rebecca Rolls Out of Town

Rebecca walked over to the mill just as the third shift was ending to let a few work friends know that she was leaving for good. She had made a firm decision to leave. *What am I doing here? Now that I've been cut loose from my job, I have no ties to this old town...other than Mikage.* For the third day in a row, dark fast-moving clouds poured rain on streets. She wondered why after ten years, no one in management wanted to talk with her about her work in progress, to tie up loose ends. Recent production on a new paperboard product was running way below specs on moisture. She had made notes to raise concerns to her supervisor's attention. No one seemed to care.

During her ten years at the mill, she had made improvements first in scheduling, and then in quality control. She had turned the quality control lab into a super efficient inspection and testing department—now she was leaving without a chance to wrap up. Anyone who had a practical operating knowledge of the mill knew she would be sorely missed. Her approach was to make sure that the paperboard manufacturing processes met industry standards and customer requirements; nothing more or less. She sampled production runs, and made sure that all of the instruments in the lab were calibrated and maintained. She seldom requested new equipment because she liked to use the traditional instruments, many of which dated back to the 1930s when the mill was first built. When she had worked in scheduling, she designed and built a customized slide rule that could calculate and optimize the trim width of the paperboard machine with different-sized orders.

The folks at the mill had arranged an impromptu going away party for Rebecca in the basement break room. The mill manager heard about the gathering and thought it would be a good idea to make an appearance. On the way, he stopped by the quality lab and grabbed her hand-made slide rule. He presented the rule to her as a going away gift (she was the only one who knew how it worked). Someone passed around home-made cookies and lemonade first intended for someone else's birthday.

"Rebecca, things won't be the same here without you—," the mill manager began. Those were the last words Rebecca heard. Afraid that she would scream again, she started counting backwards from one hundred by sevens, then passed out. All those years, she had been as reliable as one of her well-maintained lab instruments—accurate, precise, and predictable—the same role she had played in her family. But this day she broke down. When she regained consciousness, David raised her to her feet, steadied her, and drove her home. He placed her slide rule, and a bag of cookies in the back seat. When he parked the car outside her apartment, he wrote his phone number on a scrap of paper.

"Here, take this and call me if you want."

"Okay."

"Would you like me to walk you up the stairs?"

"No, thank you."

"Rebecca."

"Bye, David."

***

In the evening, Rebecca walked over to Mikage's place for dinner. Mikage was busy behind the counter with her head down plating a meal. Rebecca watched a Latina mother and three children eat an early lunch in the booth behind her. A little toddler girl placed macaroni curls over each of the finger tips of one hand, and examined her new fingernails. As her older sister looked on with disgust, the toddler began licking a cheesy elbow from each finger until her mother noticed what she was doing. Her infant brother chuckled during the scolding. Mikage chatted with the woman in fluent Spanish. In another booth, two pierced teenage boys, sheathed in tattoos, sipped Cokes. When Mikage was free to talk, Rebecca told her that she had decided to leave town.

"Why are you doing this?!" said Mikage.

"There's nothing left for me here."

"I suppose you know I'll miss you," said Mikage.

"I'll come back to see you."

"Please don't forget me."

"Of course I won't." Rebecca placed her hand on Mikage's shoulder.

"Promise?"

"Promise."

Just then, the little Latina girl knocked her mother's coffee cup onto the floor. It shattered. Mikage walked over to pick up the pieces and cradled them in her half apron. She told the mother not to worry. Then she placed the broken pieces in a box. "I never throw broken things away," she said, "you can always find another use." Rebecca noticed Mikage's little art objects behind the counter—made from broken cups, saucers, and dishes.

"That box looks like me," Rebecca said.

"Nonsense. We are strong women. When we have problems, we figure things out and move on. Find something to do that makes you happy."

"David told me to try fishing."

"Maybe you should try fishing."

Mikage cracked two eggs into a glass bowl, turned over the hash on the grill with a large spatula, and began to prepare Rebecca's breakfast. Mikage fixed Rebecca poached eggs over homemade corned beef hash with small blueberry pancakes on the side. As she served the meal, she said, "You need more meat on your bones, and only God knows when you'll get a proper meal again."

When Rebecca had finished eating, Mikage presented Rebecca with a black lacquered wooden bento box to take with her. The inside of the box was colored red, filled with California rolls filled with cucumber, avocado, and crab meat surrounded by an outside layer of rice and sprinkled with sesame seeds. Because Mikage was so short and Rebecca so tall, Rebecca knelt to receive her gift.

After securing another promise to stay in touch, Mikage looked up at Rebecca with glossy dark eyes. Composing herself, she said, "I will miss you very much, but I know you need to find a happier place."

"I want a home like I used to have."

"Work is not home."

"I know."

Then Mikage came around the counter with an untroubled smile, and hugged Rebecca around the waist so tight she couldn't breathe. Mikage hugged her for the longest time, mumbling, "I love you" and "my angel" over and over. Then she drew back into her work. Rebecca could not match Mikage's emotional intensity.

The two women eyed each other one more time, and then went on about their business, foregoing farewells as if they would continue seeing each other every day for the rest of their lives.

****

The Lawnmower Club: How Leo Zitzelberger Lost and Found Paradise on Earth
(an excerpt from Red Sky Series, Book 4)

Prologue

Six in the morning. The cougar moves soft-footed through the wood's edge. In the red dawn light of summer, the air trembles around him.

To small forest creatures, he looks like a never-ending procession of sun-flecked fur trailing a long upturned tail. Seven feet long— beautiful and brutal, he threshes the brush under spruce boughs. The primitive landscape of his new territory would be perfect, except for the nonstop thrumming of lawnmower engines.

The cougar raises an eyebrow as he looks beyond a stand of cedars on the other side of a swamp where the unfathomable noise starts at first light and doesn't stop until just before sundown, six days a week. Sunday stays silent as deep forest. Monday mornings, the unnatural lawnmower sounds once again disturb the primal stillness.

The Wisconsin cougar had escaped over an ice bridge to the northern Lower Peninsula of Michigan before the early spring thaw. The rich land provides the large predator with an abundant supply of rabbits, woodcock, turkey, porcupines, raccoons, coyotes, deer—and numberless chipmunk, his favorite snack when he wants a little something. The cougar could have ranged deeper into state park land nearby, but the sure source of easy prey keeps him in this unfamiliar 30-square mile territory. A Garden of Eden—except for the unnatural and incomprehensible noise from a small army of lawnmower engines.

The cougar stops to collect his motions into shape, then stares in the direction of the noise. He smells gas fumes and engine oil. There is a magical intelligence behind his face and eyes. His broad range of vision picks up several men riding lawnmowers over a savannah of green grass. His body tenses. He launches terrible hisses in the direction of the lawnmowers, showing his teeth and superb gum health, the last thought of the dental hygienist he'd recently attacked in Wisconsin. *Why did she wear red running shoes? I hate red. Now humans want my hide.*

The cougar runs off across a dirt road, over an embankment, and deep into the underbrush. He's light on his feet and lightning fast. But even at a distance, the lawnmower noise lingers over the fields. The mechanical sounds encroach the cougar's world as strange. The sounds disturb his thinking; makes him pace when he's awake and whimper when he's asleep. He wants either supreme quiet or the sounds of nature.

Unlike the more limited consciousness of other animals, the cougar's mental abilities excel beyond the guesswork of scientists, both a gift and burden. Or maybe he's not unique; just slightly more gifted and burdened than the rest of his species. Who knows? He possesses the gifts of reflective thought and memory and intent; the burden of negative emotions, the capacity to suffer beyond pain, and the fragile pursuit of happiness in the face of imminent death. He knows his place in nature. He tries to breathe through the racket. He summons positive thoughts. He thinks how the rebound of whitetails in North America has supported his independent lifestyle. His muscles relax.

The cougar lives in an abandoned landfill site two miles from the golf course. He circles back, and uncovers a fresh deer carcass protected with deadfall limbs, a kill from the previous night. He eats without the usual pleasure; feels stressed deep inside his light-colored underbelly. *It will do me good to roam*, he thinks. He takes a walk on the nature trail nearby, drinks swirling algae-flecked water from a creek.

The cougar returns to his daybed in the landfill. He stretches and yawns and closes his eyes for a morning catnap. Little lives scurry all around him, playing chicken to see who can come closest. The critters never get used to seeing him. The cougar is almost as strange to them, as the lawnmower riders are to the cougar.

During his twitchy dreams, the cougar pounces with vampire bites to the necks of the riders like he's sinking his teeth in a juicy rabbit. The thrill of the ambush stirs through his best nighttime reveries. During the daytime, the noise infuriates the cougar. Could he get close enough to the mowers for a sneak attack? The golf course's expanse of cut grass provides no cover.

He decides to hunt. His life would be so empty without something to kill—the blessing and curse of a natural predator.

Chapter One
The Cart Shed

Leo Zitzelberger opens his eyes on an ordinary summer day. He thinks that he might be the luckiest man on earth.

Waking at nine from his morning nap, he yawns and stretches his long arms and legs. He rises slowly from the slider on the clubhouse deck to watch the morning riders on the golf course he now calls home. He pours a large cup of lukewarm coffee. He yawns again—his yellow teeth jutting out from shrunken gums, a dental hygienist's nightmare. He opens a cookie tin and removes the last bit of a blueberry muffin from its paper doily, his favorite snack when he wants a little something. He tears away a piece of muffin from its stretchy, donut-like top and pops it into his mouth. The taste is not nearly as good as the muffins that Mona, his deceased wife, had baked from scratch on Sunday mornings.

Remembrances of Mona come less frequently these days. The change of locations has helped. For a long time after she died, his consciousness had been split between "before Mona" and "after Mona," but his lawn mowing club has offered him a new life, not as good as the old one, but acceptable, tolerable, and digestible like a store-bought blueberry muffin.

As he finishes the last crumb, he remembers an important task. *Oh, yes, a new lawnmowerian has applied for membership today.* He must interview him before the first shift—one of his duties as owner and founder of The Lawnmower Club.

In the red sky of morning, Zitzelberger carries his large body over to the old cart shed to inspect the new member's lawn tractor. He walks east into the red morning sun, dragging his shadow like a black cape—like a character created for a novel. A tall healthy 65-year-old except for bulk, his feet leave large footprints in the sandy soil. He passes a boxlike, glassed-in sign, the kind you find displaying a sermon topic in front of a country church. The sign reads, *"NO CHILDREN, NO PETS!"* He pauses and bends reverently before entering the dim light of the cart shed, as if he's stepping into the tabernacle of a sanctified sect. He smells the sweet incense of grease, gas, and mildew.

In some ways, he's like a priest. He leads a celibate and solitary life, dedicated to cutting grass and maintaining his independence. He stands over six feet tall with a hatchet face and large steel-colored eyes. His sharp chin looks like the toe of a Western dress boot. When he walks, his arms swing like the blades of a chain saw. To people in town he looks fearsome—mothers pick up their children when he lumbers down the sidewalk. Dog owners heel their dogs. Boys laugh or throw stones at him. In Zitzelberger's mind, the perfect town would be one with a few shops along brick-red streets, a large grassy village green with a flag pole, and no people.

Most of the town people hold grudges against Zitzelberger for relieving them of the burdens of car ownership. Before he retired, Zitzelberger owned a car repo agency, and hauled away cars when people couldn't make their car payments. Popular only with bank collectors and finance companies, people who hate him dot his life like dandelions on an otherwise perfect lawn.

Zitzelberger wants to make sure the new member is a good fit——that he possesses true *lawnmowerian* values—a love of grass, respect for machines, and a do-it-yourself mentality. He only wants people as members who never get bored making straight-cut rows and running their machines. And people who don't want to turn the club into anything else. If a prospective member asks, "What else can we do with our membership besides cut grass? Could we have picnics with our family, play horseshoes, or camp?" All knockout factors. He only wants members who desire to mow grass—who are obsessed by grass cutting; who don't even daydream while cutting, because there is nothing more engaging or satisfying or exciting than cutting grass.

Now he walks catlike by rows of lawnmowers, and wrecks of other machinery that members could not part with when they lost their homes: weed eaters, hedge trimmers, power edgers, leaf blowers, uprooted sprinkler systems, log splitters, air compressors, dethatchers, front-end loaders, and spreader attachments. Zitzelberger has no rules about storing extra equipment as long as there's room in the cart barn. He's unusually liberal in this regard. *Men need their machines,* he thinks.

Each member has a dedicated work space where they can place their workbenches like altars. On peg board above the benches t squares hang like crosses, and socket wrenches lay on top like communion candlesticks; everything necessary for maintenance on their mowers. Zitzelberger doesn't allow family photographs or trophies or service club plaques. No pinup calendars or other ephemera clutter the sacred space. But yellowed diagrams and posters of lawnmower engines and mowers are fine, or clipboards of maintenance records and instruction manuals.

If someone has a non-mower-related hobby of any kind, from woodworking to building model ships, Zitzelberger says, *"YOU CAN PLAY WITH THOSE THINGS AT THE SENIOR CENTER!"* He allows no drinking or smoking in the cart shed. *"NO CHILDREN, NO PETS!" I want a fixed focus on lawn mowing in my club. No distractions. Purity. Simplicity. Dedication.*

He walks quietly up behind the new member, as if he intends to scare the *bejeezus* out of him, which is exactly what he is doing. He wants to catch him off guard, a test for healthy reflexes. *"LOOKS LIKE A SCAG!"* he speaks in a low rolling rumble like the sound of distant thunder.

He develops a good first impression, not of the man, but of his machine. It looks clean and oiled, a V-Ride with a Stripe Roller. Zitzelberger had read about this bright new orange model—a Cheetah 61-inch zero-turn rider with a fast, air-cooled 36-horse-power engine.

The new member turns to Zitzelberger, and tries not to act startled. "Yep, I've always had Scags, every model they ever made: Turf Tigers, Tiger Cubs, Saber Tooth Tigers, and the Wildcat—now that was a great cutter. But this new Cheetah is the best! Runs up to 16 miles per hour!" As he moves his hands with love over his lawn tractor's steering wheel, the new member grins a gold tooth at Zitzelberger. Zitzelberger raises his eyebrow, but decides to smile back, even though he regards smiling as a sign of weakness. He parts his lips slowly, as if he's opening a wound.

"Mow for a living?" Zitzelberger says.

"No, but like most of the folks here, I live to mow. I'm a residential mower, but I have always wanted commercial grade equipment—needed to keep moving up, one model one make at a time, you know. Kept buying bigger properties for more grass to cut. Then my kids moved me into an old folk's home surrounded by lousy, neglected landscaping. I'm sure you can imagine the torture—confining a *lawn man* to a place surrounded by an unkempt yard or no yard at all. I sat by the window looking outside all day, and couldn't stop thinking about my tractor sitting unused and unmaintained in my daughter's garage. So sad. But then I heard about this place—what a great idea! You're a savior of sorts—"

Zitzelberger detects a tone of self-pity. He hates expressions of either positive or negative emotions. Happy or sad equally offend him. "—I don't care to hear people's sob stories, and I don't regard myself as anybody's savior," Zitzelberger interjects. "I need members to help pay the bills so I can live the way I want to live. You're not the first man to lose his home, and you won't be the last." Zitzelberger locks his eyes on the new member like a large predator about to take prey. The new member's eyes widen white like broken eggshells.

"I want people who pay their dues, keep their assigned shifts, and run their machines properly without damaging the turf. This isn't a church or a bridge club. We're all here to mow, and I want people who mow grass well.

"Go ahead and tell me a little about your mowing history, since I have to evaluate you. But if I accept you, I don't care to hear any more about your past. Some of the members may want to trade stories about the good or bad old days, but I'm not interested in what you did way back when or what happened. Memories are like a rotten-smelling mower bag of old clippings."

The new mowers face freezes and his skin turns to parchment. Zitzelberger thinks he may have come on too strong, which he did.

"Now I can tell by the look on your face that you think I'm coming on a bit harsh. I'm just making myself clear, see. *"MOW HERE NOW"*—that's my motto. So go on. Tell me the headlines—like the front-page of the *Petoskey News & Review*."

The prospective member clears his throat like he's about to make a life or death statement. Now his entire body appears jagged, frozen, and tilted backwards away from Zitzelberger. "Well, I do think I can make a lawn look better than the next guy—I take good care of the blades and the deck. But I like the ride more than anything. Can you believe they're making robot mowers now?" The man had spent so much time in the sun that his face and arms are covered with sun damage and scars from melanoma surgery. He gives Zitzelberger another please-like-me smile.

"Well, I've heard remotes work for steep hills and ditches," Zitzelberger says, "but I like to haul tail on an incline myself. I hate hedge trimmers and weed eaters; hate shrubby lawns. I like grass right up to the foundation. Pure grass, green grass that's been cared for, and cut by someone with skill. Not everyone can afford a big house, but everyone can have a well-tended lawn. I like to walk around a lawn in my bare feet and get fresh clippings in between my toes." The new mower glimpses a glimmer of encouragement in Zitzelberger's eyes.

"You'll see...I'm not at the end of my mowing career." the new member says, "Someday I want to get the 72-inch Scag with a bigger engine—maybe used if it looks like new and the compression test—"

"—check the maintenance records," Zitzelberger cuts in. "Make sure you have the receipts, especially for new parts. You need lawnmower parts for two reasons: one of them is for simple use of the machine; the other is the result of *hurt*. You must know the difference. You shouldn't hurt machines. I bet you know that.'"

"Sure 'nough." The two men achieve a beginner's level of mutual respect.

"Well, you pass. I'll let you into the club next Tuesday after your check clears. Now, here are the ground rules. Even though this is no longer a golf course, I want it to *look* like one—green, lush, well-kept. I'll expect you to keep your shift. When you ride, keep your balance on the seat, avoid spinning your tires, and if you do dig into muddy spots or standing water, let me know. Another thing, report broken sprinkler heads—I have some boys who can replace them, but I've gotta know."

"Thanks for letting me in!" the new member says. "You'll like my mowing style. I'm a good chopper, and keep the clippings cleaned from under the deck. I started out with a push reel mower when I was a kid (still have it). In the '50s, I bought a Briggs and Stratton on a Cooper aluminum deck (back when they built 'em in the USA)—later used the engine to run my son's Go-Kart. My son ran it into a creek. He drowned...but I fished out the engine (it was under water *nine hours* hydro-locked!)—still runs on the first pull—have the owner's manual, too. In the '60s, I upgraded to a 1962 Toro Reel with a Wisconsin engine. I know it's an art form—like the other grass cutters here. *MOWING IS A JOURNEY WITH NO DESTINATION.*"

"Yep," says Zitzelberger, "I admit that's a nice statement even though you dredged up a bit of the past which I just told you holds no interest for me. But think about it...this used to be a golf course crawling with people who shirked their yard work to play an impossible game that does violence to grass. Now let me remind you one more time, no more stories about the past or about journeys and destinations, at least not to me."

"Oh, my prayers have been answered!" the new member says.

"If prayer did any good, they'd pay people to do it...I mean pay big bucks...and we'd all get dropped ass-first into paradise. FAT CHANCE!"

Zitzelberger relishes his life of freedom living at the The Lawnmower Club. He bought the property at a bank sale five years earlier after Mona died. He sold her business, Mona Lease-a-Car. He listed their home. He couldn't stay around the place any longer with Mona gone. The house had felt deserted. As the months passed, the light bulbs popped and fizzled out one-by-one. He didn't replace them. His insides felt like the burnt-out bulbs looked—a black residue at the bottom of a glassy, bulbous enclosure. The first lights to go lit the spaces he and Mona had spent most time together—the family room floods, the florescent lights in the kitchen; then the bedroom lamps—until after sundown, he sat in the dark.

The night Mona died had been dark from a dome of clouds that hung over the yard all day. Even though he worked outside from morning to evening, there always seemed to be one more thing to do before Mona called him in for dinner. After he went inside, they would eat mostly in silence. When they did talk, controversial subjects were out of the question. Zitzelberger had been raised not to argue at the dinner table or risk a beating by his father. So they conversed politely in private like they were sitting in a restaurant where all could hear. Mona was a meat and potatoes cook, and Zitzelberger liked what she fixed. Eating and talking were too much for him, so he concentrated on eating. It hadn't always been that way, but after so many years, their marriage had drifted into mutual silence. Mona was like the air he breathed. The air didn't need his attention, and neither did she.

This dark night, Zitzelberger noticed that Mona hadn't called him in for dinner. His yard had nearly disappeared against the fast-dimming sky. He barged through the screen door yelling for her. Mona was nowhere, until he found her at the bottom of the basement stairs lying on her back with her neck broken and no heart beat. Why she had decided to go to the basement he had no idea. He called an ambulance. He had never been so distressed. When they wheeled her away, he began to miss her with an ache that would ache every day for the rest of his life.

And with Mona's death, the comfortable division of labor they had shared crumbled. He had to either take care of everything on the inside and outside, or choose to ignore certain things. He chose to ignore the inside—the inside of the house and the inside of him. He spent most of the time outside on his porch or in the yard or in his detached garage. He tried to walk away from his past like it had belonged to someone else.

During the months after Mona's death, his vibrant green and well-tended lawn provided his sole consolation. If he had been zealous about lawn care before Mona died, caring for his lawn grew into a greater obsession. He sat on his front porch all day, guarding the lawn and glaring at people passing by when he wasn't directly tending it. When he left for town to do errands, he stuck a large sign in the turf: *"KEEP OFF THE LAWN!"*

A mean streak in his personality rarely surfaced while Mona had lived, and outbursts quickly faded when Mona kindly said, "Now, Leo…" But after her death, Zitzelberger couldn't seem to back off his meanness. He had to do something different. He wanted something else, but he didn't know what.

There was something better. He purchased a bankrupt golf course and formed a club for men who loved to cut grass, but had lost their yards. Now every day except Sunday the same. Mowers arrive at first light to mow in two-hour shifts. For a $1,000 initiation fee plus annual dues of $1,000, the mowers mount riding machines stabled in the old cart barn, and mow their assigned fairway plots. With 27 holes and four mowers per fairway one day per week, his total membership of 100 has almost reached capacity in less than a year.

Zitzelberger can't believe his good fortune—his whole world filled with the hum of engines, and the sweet fumes of lawnmower exhaust. From behind the large windows on the second floor deck of the clubhouse, he keeps his eyes on ten members raising little dust clouds, sitting fixed on their mowers. The old men mowing look straight ahead like the terra cotta warriors of a Chinese emperor.

Zitzelberger laughs at the sight, because it makes him feel like royalty: *"I'm the King of Geezerdom! My subjects get to ride out the tail end of their lives on big grass-cutting machines. My life is no longer declining. I'm changing directions."*

Zitzelberger loves to walk from one end of the vast pole barn to the other for his daily inspections. Every model and make of lawn tractor sits in neat rows from one end to the other: front-mounted engine models with side discharges, zero-turn radius mowers with rear-wheel steering, big rear baggers, and heavy-duty tractors. Members ask him questions about starters, primers, switches, carburetors, governors, oil and gas leaks, spark plugs, mufflers, crankshaft repairs, and blade sharpening. He interprets instruction manuals like a holy man reveals the truths of sacred texts. As long as people stay on topic, he enjoys his rounds. He's even patient when a member uses the word "doohickey" to describe a part.

In the beginning, the members want to have meetings to make rules and air grievances. Zitzelberger hates meetings. One of the members in particular has a personal agenda. Hazard Pembrook, a fortyish third-generation resorter, wants to impose a dress code to restore the decorum of the old days when his parents owned the property as a private haven for rich golfers. "Proper mowing attire is as important as proper grass," he says. "You need to ride in style. Other people can look like slobs, but not a crackerjack grass cutter!"

Pembrook constantly studies the dress of people around him for signs of bad taste and indecency, people whose membership applications would have been rejected by his father who golfed in tweeds and knickers, who dressed for dinner until the day he died, and who told Pembrook when he was a boy to never wear anything that looked like it could be purchased in a department store.

"Locals!" his father would say haughtily as he looked at new applications to the country club. "Why do they bother to apply? They're not *our* kind of people."

Pembrook mows in a wool sports coat with arm patches, canvas hunting pants and high-laced boots. He listens to Bach on a headset. He lives alone in a rambling Victorian mansion across the street from the club where stand-up mirrors appear in every room like Stations of the Cross. He's a trust fund baby. His father had been a trust fund baby. He wants to be the mirror image of his father—not his grandfather, who had worked for a living. His grandfather made money in the railroad business, and portraits hanging on the walls in Pembrook's house show a tiny man hunched over from carrying bags of money to the bank. Pembrook has never worked for money. He doesn't like to get his hands dirty. He always wears gloves.

Pembrook regards his well-maintained, comely lawn as a status symbol, a way to distinguish the upper class from farmers who need their land to grow crops; a way to make neighbors with lesser lawns look inferior and proletarian by comparison. Also, as a single man recently divorced, he thinks, *with an immense lawn I feel more marriageable.* He also likes the security afforded by a large lawn where intruders lack the benefit of cover, and predators cannot mount sneak attacks.

"I can see all the way to Wisconsin from my house," he says. "I feel safe knowing what may be coming from afar. In this wild section of the country, who knows what may be lurking in the cover of wilderness? Perhaps native peoples once occupied this sacred hill where they could see pirates, missionaries, mammoths, and saber-toothed tigers approaching from afar."

Pembrook has a lawn service do his own yard across the street from the club. He joined The Lawnmower Club, because he wanted something manly to do during the day. He also wanted to belong because of his happy memories there. His family had owned the property through his childhood, the best stage of his life. He used to hang around the clubhouse, and practice putting and chipping along with other "junior" members. He never developed enough coordination to be a golfer, but he liked the ambience of the place.

He still longs for those halcyon days when lazy children were tolerated in the privileged class he represented. Those were my days of *"splendor in the grass,"* he would say fondly during occasional summer cocktail parties on his expansive front porch. When he made the statement, he would look across to the acres of fairways with wistful eyes, a look he occasionally practiced in the stand-up mirrors.

Rory Finnegan, another member, serves as Pembrook's foil. A large man with red hair, he grips the wheel of his lawn tractor one-handed with the vise grip of an Olympic wrestler, which he once was. In the other hand, he holds a fly swatter, and slaps away at the little pesks as he mows. His large feet rest on the mower housing like two boxes of cement. He smokes big black cigars and mows shirtless in grass-stained shorts. His torso front and back is hairy as a bear.

Finnegan made his money on his own, and has little respect for "the upper classes." He's a man's man in every way. He regards Pembrook with the disinterested respect he applies to all people. He knows that Pembrook thinks he's too "blue collar," but he doesn't give a rat's ass. He likes to say, "What people think of me is none of my business." Finnegan likes to mow early in the morning when he can hear every part of his machine singing like a chorus grinding out "When Irish Eyes Are Smiling."

Harold Peter Custer, a well-off retired automobile mogul, prefers to mow barefoot in his flannel pajamas with a wide-brimmed straw hat. Like most of his fellow members, he regards lawn mowing to be a fine art. He gives frequent advice to others: "You need to cut when the grass is dry," he says in his raspy voice. "I don't care how big your machine or what make, wet grass sticks and clogs a grass cutting machine, and puts extra strain on the parts." Custer sings as he mows: "*The breeze is a-blowin, the grass won't stop growin, oh, mowin the lawn, mowin the lawn, it's what I gotta do, listen to the sound, rev it up, take it down, it's what I gotta do, mowin the lawn, mowin the lawn.*"

Custer had lost his driver's license when he turned 85 because of an unfortunate accident. He coincidentally injured or killed two hunters, a game warden, and a deer when he veered off the road while eating fast food. He arrives for his mowing shift at The Lawnmower Club in a chauffeured sunflower yellow limousine with six wheels—long, sleek, fast, and low to the ground. His chauffeur reaches into the back seat with both arms and pulls Custer to a standing position where he remains until he gains his balance. The great-great grandson of the famous general, he surveys the mowers riding their machines like he's looking for Lakota Sioux and Cheyenne warriors about to attack. He's the man with the most money, and he has the biggest machine: a John Deere four-wheel drive model 8800 Terrain Cut with a 42-horsepower diesel engine and five floating decks. "The cutting decks reticulate to hold the contours of the ground," he says proudly. "By George, they use one on the National Mall in Washington, D.C!"

Other issues arise among the *lawnmowerians*: proposals for standard bench settings for cutting height, cuts per yard of grass, safety training and protective gear, bagging and dumping practices, security for the lawnmower shed. Zitzelberger has no interest in democratic processes within his world. He didn't found the club to hear squabbles. The last straw: someone proposes a social membership for non-riding walkers. Zitzelberger shuts down the meetings; allows one every five years; hopes he will die before the next one.

After the orientation session, Zitzelberger returns to his slider and reclines while eyeing the large computer screen showing the GPS location of all the mowers represented by little red rectangles—two working the far edges of each fairway. He loves the new cloud-based farm management software a sales rep sold him. He tracks all the field activities: the moisture content of each area, the topsoil and subsoil pH, and detailed logs of what was done on each fairway: de-thatching records, re-grassing projects, organic fertilization, weed, insect, and varmint control, sprinkler maintenance, and damage repair areas (no longer caused by cart tracks, ball marks, golf shoes, or temper tantrums). He plans his improvements on his bathroom throne reading his bibles: *Month-by-Month Lawn Care* and *The Encyclopedia of Turf Management.*

After a full day, he moves to his bedroom on the second floor of the clubhouse for the night. A recent visit from a social worker has troubled his sleep lately.

She wants to put him away in Mallard Pond, an old folks home no better than a prison. He looks up at the ceiling, wishing the visit was a distant memory, rather than something that had happened a couple days earlier. He can't stop the scene looping through his head.

Chapter Two
The Social Worker

Near lunchtime, Zitzelberger sizzles burgers on his charcoal grill, while Jimmy Buffet's "Cheeseburgers in Paradise" plays on his old stereo. Blue smoke rises skyward, and sifts sunlight like a peace offering to another day in his personal version of paradise on earth. He munches softly on a handful of stale potato chips, and listens to the pleasant hiss of fat dropping from the hefty burgers onto the white hot coals.

Satisfied that the burgers are on their way to perfection, he melts into his leopard spots print lawn chair. The canvas enfolds him like the skin of a cat, like someone had sewn him in. He reads a story in the local newspaper. He mouths what he reads, as if words of his own making are the only ones worthy of trust.

"*Shrubbery!*" He reads an article about the benefits of living in a retirement community. "*Shrubbery*" happens to be Zitzelberger's favorite curse word, particularly when he's in high dudgeon.

"There are so many things to hate about shrubs," he had told a club member. "Shrubs scratch and poke people, shrubs hide robbers, and bring deer up to the house. People trim and fuss with shrubbery to impress their neighbors when they should be maintaining their lawns. 'Grass right up to the foundations,' that's what I say. I feel the same about flowers, except shrubs are worse! Shrubs and hedges are a way to divide people and turf—without shrubbery, we'd have fewer wars!"

Without warning, a social worker barges into his backyard with the results of her independent living assessment. She drags a rolling backpack through the gravel. Gloria Fitting has high cheek bones and a prominent nose. She's tall and skinny as a shadow, and her long legs seem to go high up making her look stork-like.

Even though she's only 25-years-old, she looks like an old woman. She wears her dark brown hair topped off in a bun like a ball of yarn with loose strands escaping. Her frizzly hair bun looks shrubby to Zitzelberger. An oversized vintage sweater drapes her body like a tea cozy.

Zitzelberger looks at her sideways with the stiff neck of an old man.

The girl with the bun doesn't give Zitzelberger a chance to react. She begins in a nasal voice without looking at him, as she hunches over her clipboard. Zitzelberger doesn't know what to make of her. Ever since losing his wife, he's lived deep down in the society of men.

"You!" says Zitzelberger contemptuously. *"Who are you?"* He unwraps himself slowly from his cocoon.

The social worker looks up briefly over her black boxy glasses that are falling down her nose, then looks back down at the clip board, thick with dog-eared papers, "Mr. Zitzelberger, my name is Gloria Fitting. I'm here to help you. I have received orders from the county to investigate your independent living skills. The county has responded to telephone calls from concerned parties." She paces back and forth like a zoo animal.

Gloria knows she's on shaky ground and uses the word "orders" to add weightiness to her statement. Pembrook had called the county saying he was concerned about a destitute neighbor living across the street in an "abandoned" clubhouse. He portrayed Zitzelberger as an eccentric hermit who couldn't take care of himself. Pembrook can't get over his resentment about his family's loss of the golf that his family had owned for most of its long history. "Even though we had to sell the place...I feel like I still own it in my heart," he would say to people with sad eyes, which he can totally pull off because he practices.

It was at the golf club that Pembrook had his only brush with honest work when his father suggested that he caddy. As soon as young Pembrook discovered that a golf caddy was required to walk long distances while carrying other people's luggage like a bellhop, he used his ample allowance to hire his own bag carrier. His father relieved him of the position at the request of the head of the golf committee. "I sliced a tee shot deep into the woods, and said to your son, 'Boy, go find my ball." You won't believe what he said. He said, 'Sir, you have no idea what dangerous predators may be lurking in those faraway woods...and besides, don't you find looking for lost balls a bit plebeian?' Well, I couldn't hit another ball squarely for the rest of my round. I started thinking about my lost golf ball, and wild animals in the woods. He threw me off my game."

Pembrook does his best to describe Zitzelberger as feeble and inept. "The man's sixty-five, but he looks a hundred with his saggy neck folds," Pembrook had said. "He doesn't look like himself, you know, like a dead man in a casket. He doesn't know how to dress, and he never goes out. I can't begin to fathom his eating habits. Oh yes, it's my civic duty to report him like the Good Samaritan did on the road to...I can't remember.

Mind you, I have no ulterior motives...only pure selfless regard for others. But do let me know when you remove him, because I would like to take the property off his hands. The proceeds could provide funds for his care, although he's not long for this world. Oh, Damascus...the Parable of the Highway to Damascus, that's it...you know, in the New Testament...or maybe the Testament before that...the older one."

Pembrook sees himself more as an honorary proprietor than a member of The Lawnmower Club. He doesn't feel he belongs to the general category of the club's *lawnmowerians*—he's more refined, genteel. He doesn't live to mow like the others. But mowing is something he can do, as long as his machine doesn't break down. He's not mechanical—his family had always hired people to do that sort of thing.

As Gloria talks, Zitzelberger's face turns the gray of cement, and he slits his eyes. *"Um, hah, I bet I know who called the county...yeah, I bet I know who...I'll be sure to give him a piece of mind. You bet I will!"*

"Confidential." Gloria hunches back down over her clipboard. "Now, after my first meeting with you, I did an assessment. Your score indicates that your independent living skills are far below what is required to live here on your own. Mr. Zitzelberger, you need assistance."

"Why?" asks Zitzelberger. He rises too abruptly from the sling chair, and topples over into a heap. His drugstore reading glasses fall off. He knocks over a wrought iron table by the grill, spilling potato chips on the ground, a sweating stack of cheddar cheese, and his man-sized spatula and tongs. He sits on the ground with his legs raised in the air like he's fallen down in the middle of a yard sale. Sheets of newspaper blow away like scattering geese.

"As I said, Mr. Zitzelberger, you scored below the acceptable limits on what we call ADL's. When you live alone at your age, you are always one step away from disaster. It's a good thing I'm here to help you up." She bends over to help him up.

"*I CAN GET UP ON MY OWN...*and I wouldn't have fallen if it hadn't been for you caterwauling around my property like a wild animal. Now what did you say about an ADL?"

"An ADL is a series of scales for 'activities of daily living.' An ADL score takes about 15 minutes to figure. I learned how to do it in school with case studies and role plays. You have serious deficits in hygiene, food preparation, dressing, paying bills, and housekeeping. In other words, you're a mess."

Zitzelberger raises his bushy eyebrows, and looks at her closely. "I thought living long enough might put me in a special category, one that gives me a pass on monkey business like this. How do you think I survived this long? I do just fine on my own, and besides, you work for the county, don't you. Well, I pay taxes for the services I need like snowplowing the roads, but I don't need your services. *No-Sir-Ree-Bob!* I don't need your help, now move along and—*"DON'T SCREW WITH MY LIFE!"*

He stands before her in a state of self indictment wearing his moth-eaten cardigan buttoned crookedly and green, grease-stained corduroys; standing in front of a stack of unpaid bills on the dirty picnic table behind him, while putrid odors drift through a kitchen screen door unhinged at the top.

"You don't have to yell at me. I'll have you know I'm very sensitive to criticism," Gloria says. "I don't see why you don't let me help you. It's for your own good, you know. You should trust me, because I'm a social worker."

"*Shrubbery!*" Zitzelberger says. "Why should I trust you because you're a social worker? You want to funnel me into a nursing home. I wouldn't fit in there. I have never fit in anywhere. That's why I live *here.*"

"Mr. Zitzelberger, you're looking at me like you think I'm nuts. I'm serious. I've reviewed your file with my supervisor, and we both agree an *intervention* is necessary. You need professional care."

"*Oh yeah...well who's going to take care of my club?*" he says. "*Tell me that!*" He makes a wide sweeping motion in the direction of the fairways. "*I won't let anyone take me away from here...OVER MY DEAD BODY!*"

"I'm surprised at you, Mr. Zitzelberger, because it says in my psychology textbook that people your age become more agreeable and compliant."

"We only get angry when we're intimidated. You're the one to blame. You're making me mildly insane. Now be a nice girl and go along and bother someone else."

"You'll live longer in a controlled environment. You need to imagine yourself into a retirement home."

"You have to have a reason to keep living," he says. "Put me in Mallard Pond, and I'll die in a matter of weeks," he snarls like a wild animal. His overlarge dark eyes look fearsome underneath his bushy eyebrows and his brow furrows. His fists clench and his back muscles tense like he might pounce on the skinny, young social worker.

Suddenly he thinks what Mona would say if she were standing beside him, "Now, Leo, calm down. This young lady's only trying to help." Of course, if Mona were here, a social worker wouldn't be coming around. Mona was the kind of all-purpose wife a man dreams of having. With their cozy little home, he took care of the outside, and she took care of the inside. Why did she fall down those steps?

Gloria Fitting continues, "Mr. Zitzelberger, you don't have what we call a social network. Without close daily connections, you'll die sooner alone than living in a place like Mallard Pond with others. Mallard Pond has all kinds of fun activities like balloon volleyball, a bus to take you shopping at Meier's and Walmart twice a week, and even Pal, a Pitt Bull therapy dog.

They also have wonderful drugs for your agitation. In a matter of hours, you'll never want to be out of there, go out, or outside, or anywhere again!"

"WOULD YOU PLEASE LEAVE ME ALONE!"

"Mr. Zitzelberger, don't be mean to me." Gloria sneezes. (She's allergic to grass and her face begins to turn splotchy.)

"Go away and leave me alone! You're sneezing on my burgers." Zitzelberger turns his back on her. His burgers are getting overdone. He cuts sweaty slabs of Velveeta, and drops them on the burgers. Over the smoke and grease, Zitzelberger smells a lingering scent of mothballs from Gloria's consignment store clothes. *"Aren't you gone yet?"* he says without looking.

"I'll go now, but I'll be back...you'll see. You're way up there on my list of difficult clients, but I won't give in." She runs away quickly, bumping into a free-range grocery cart filled with Zitzelberger's deposit bottles, her braided bun bobbing, looking white in the outdoor light like large bunny tail. Tears trail from dark eyeliner over her pale face. She hasn't eaten a good meal in days, and the gusts of cooking smells from the grill are marvelous. She thinks about saving up for her own grill.

To live all alone and work a thankless, low-paying job is a trifle depressing. Her parents are both dead, and she has no brothers or sisters. She doesn't seem to fit anywhere. She wishes she had friends. Not a whole social network like her textbooks say she should have, but simply a few good friends. If she had friends, she could complain to them about Zitzelberger. Oh, how she would like a cheeseburger!

***

Waking from his midmorning nap, the cougar ranges out for a morning snack. Roosted turkeys drop down from the treetops like they've been thrown out of a low-flying plane. There's safety in numbers. Unlike the cougar, the turkeys live in a community with what Gloria would call strong social ties. *It's too easy*, the cougar thinks. He decides to chase a runner—*more sporting.* Blood, bone, feathers, and flesh. So tasty. He would like to bring his prize home, but he has no one to care for.

He's a lone ranger alone in the wild. Independent living is all he knows. If he only had someone to provide for, a mate, it would give his life more meaning. *Subsistence. All I do is subsist. Such a shallow idea.* In a state of ennui, he sinks into a depression in the middle of a field. He smells an unnatural hint of hamburger smoke and a whiff of moth balls. He hears the incessant combustion of lawnmowers, as intrusive to the world of the cougar as the nasal voice of a social worker to the world of Zitzelberger's back yard.

***

Zitzelberger straightens up the clubhouse and pays his bills. Even though he has no intention of reading them, he buys impressive magazines like *National Geographic*, and strategically places them on the kitchen table and his nightstand in case he receives more unannounced visits from do-gooders like Gloria Fitting. He fights with all his might to stay out of Mallard Pond.

What he wants most out of life is to be left alone. He succeeds. He continues to improve the grounds of the former golf club—sells the triplex mowers used to close-cut the greens, the leftover merchandise in the old golf shop, the vending machines, and the greens-keeping equipment. He sells all the golf carts save one for himself. He scrubs bird turds and skunk shit off his picnic table.

After running a car repo agency for 40 years, Zitzelberger has finally found his true calling. Who would have thought that his lifelong pleasure, cutting grass, riding back and forth in neat rows, would be the sole source of his salvation? He rarely admits good fortune, but, if he could sing, he would sing; if he could write poetry, he would write poetry—however, his mind is seldom baffled by higher pursuits. He tries not to think further about Gloria Fitting, although he has occasional nightmares about hordes of social workers invading his property, harping about his lack of independent living skills, saying "we're here to help you."

Instead, he mows. He keeps his own patch of fairway near what used to be the eighteenth hole. It's big enough for a two-hour ride. He touches the electric starter on his Toro 48 Professional 8000, rolls out of the cart shed and onto the lush green fairway. The engine hums a symphony. When he engages the belt drive, he smells the mown grass exhale as it blows from the blade tips and sifts into the high-capacity collection system. He reaches his optimal ground speed of seven miles per hour. Once in a while when he moves up a slope, he might see cloud mountains moving across the sky at a casual pace, or on a turn, he might notice the bristling leaves on the ancient oak tree rising over the clubhouse.

But the attractions of nature are not important to Zitzelberger. He's never been sentimental about what he refers to as *scenery*. He's never had a happy response to the natural world, too untrimmed and wild. Even the *tick tick* of raindrops falling from one leaf to another in gentle rain irritates him. Neither does he associate the green tangy smell of cut grass with happy thoughts of past summers and weekends or the pleasures of boyhood. He grew up in a poor neighborhood in a small house with a dirt yard that he tended by making straight even lines with a rusty rake. Somehow making those neat lines made his topsy-turvy life more orderly.

Zitzelberger has never seen either ocean and only winks of the Great Lakes. In his land-based slumbers, a vast continental sea of green grass fills his best summer dreams, and snow fast-melting into grass fills his best winter dreams. His travel has been up and down rows of grass enough to circle the earth many times. The history of the human race, to Zitzelberger, is limited to man cutting grass and the grass growing back, week after week, year after year. Humans trimming nature, and nature fighting back. That's how he rolls. That's all he knows he wants.

Even if the Zitzelberger saw the shape of an angel in the clouds above the treetops, he would know that the angel was there for someone else, not him. But he never thinks of God or angels or otherworldly things, or anything positive or good. He has grass to cut.

***

Gloria Fitting persists. She doubles her efforts to have Zitzelberger moved to Mallard Pond. In the gloaming light of evening, she hides in the birches and watches Zitzelberger with her low light binoculars, hoping to catch him acting helpless and neglectful; hoping to witness some catastrophe that will prove her right and give her cause for rejoicing; see evidence of forgetfulness or something else broken in his head.

Placing Zitzelberger in Mallard Pond has become Gloria's obsession. Clearly she has jangled her mind with too much coffee and not enough food. She has no one to help her place Zitzelberger in perspective. Why can't she move on, as Zitzelberger suggested, and bother (or help) someone else? Lots of other people might appreciate her assistance. At some level, she knows that *she's* the one who needs help. But, she sees asking for help as a sign of weakness. If a social worker offered to help her, she would refuse. She lives alone, and blames her parents for everything. *Why did they have to get themselves killed in a car accident?*

Only a few blocks away from her house, she had been writing an essay in her diary about how she hated her parents when she heard the crash and sirens through her bedroom window. The car had split in half. A flatbed tow truck hauled it in pieces to a gas station parking lot in Gloria's neighborhood. She received a call from her Aunt Ratchet who had been working the night shift at the hospital. Her aunt told her everything would be okay, but Gloria had no idea what that meant. On the way home from the hospital where her parents were pronounced dead, she passed the wrecked car. Her aunt was driving, and Gloria insisted that they stop to see. Blood had exploded all over the twisted metal of the car's remains, and dripped from the spattered wreckage. Tiny blood pools blistered the asphalt. She screamed. She couldn't handle the blood.

Above all, she couldn't handle being cut loose from her parents at a time when she had spent her days and nights resisting them on every little detail of their efforts to control her life. She had been abandoned by her enemies. How could they have been so careless as to be hit by a semi at the most dangerous intersection in town? Didn't everyone know you had to be careful? Look both ways? Isn't that what they had told *her* to do? How could they get themselves killed without giving her any warning? At the hospital, they had given Gloria a plastic bag with cash and her father's watch. She placed the bag in her backpack, and carried it on her shoulders unopened for years, thinking that somehow opening it would make her parents' deaths irreversible.

Gloria had been the only child with only a single aunt in town. Her aunt had not been much help, because she had problems of her own. So Gloria finished high school living at a girl friend's house. Her girl friend's parents let her do pretty much as she pleased, but nothing pleased her. She not only blamed her parents for her unhappy life, but anyone else who happened to cross her path—especially adults. One Saturday night the police busted Gloria for underage drinking. She had downed a six-pack of beer in the back seat of a boy's car. When her girlfriend's father yelled at her, she ran away. She lived in her car for a few weeks, but ended up in the office of a social worker.

A well-dressed woman just out of college, the social worker said, "I'm your social worker. You can trust me." The way she said, "I'm your social worker," impressed Gloria, like someone on high had assigned her or given her magical powers—like an angel. Here was a confident, professional-looking woman, not that much older than herself, who wore a beeper, and seemed to know practical ways to fix people and their problems. She wore her hair in a neat bun. From that day, Gloria decided to go to college and become a social worker. She hit the books and received a scholarship.

The day she graduated from college, Gloria opened the plastic bag and took out her father's watch along with a lumpy pile of twenties, tens, fives, and ones. She put the watch on her wrist and took herself out for a graduation dinner with the cash. She ordered chicken quesadilla and a beer. If she couldn't fix her own life, she could get a salary in return for fixing other people's lives—in an air-conditioned office with her own desk and a top drawer. And she would look cool wearing a Motorola beeper and her father's Timex watch. She practiced saying, "My name is Gloria Fitting. I'm here to help you."

***

The cougar reaches the upper level of his noise tolerance. He wants to stop the noise, but he knows from his Wisconsin experience that harming humans can result in harassment or worse—getting chased by cops with dogs, darts, or bullets. He still rues the day when he attacked the dental hygienist in the red running shoes. Even though he just nicked her in the heel, he knows that to return home to Wisconsin would be suicide. He has a better plan, one that will allow him to stay unmolested by the lawnmower guys in his new home territory, but he wants to chew on his ideas. Today is silent Sunday, a quiet time for reflection. He watches a ruffed grouse trot by, but leaves the bird to its own pursuits of happiness.

***

Monday mornings, Rory Finnegan looks forward to riding out onto the wet green turf of a summer day. He wakes before dawn, arrives ahead of time to take the first shift on his Gravely ZT. His voice sounds like gravel as he speaks to the machine; sets the choke and presses the automatic starter button. As he exits the pole barn into the cool air and red sky of dawn, something doesn't feel right. He returns to the barn, opens his metal tool chest and removes his deck leveling gauge. He measures the deck side-to-side and front-to-back, checks the oil level, engages and disengages the mower blades, checks the anti-scalp rollers, the belt tension, the tire pressure.

He wipes his hands with a shop towel, and pulls up his trousers to cover his butt crack. He remounts the mower and restarts the engine. As he chugs out of the pole barn, he feels more confident about the machine, but still feels like something's not quite right, like his inner self is having wedgies. Not one to have premonitions, he thinks maybe he's just having the occasional bad day. He feels uneasy in the mower seat. Perhaps a cigar will help. He stops the Gravely, and let's the engine idle while he nips off the end of a thick torpedo-shaped cigar. He lights up with a small blow torch of a lighter, and then continues to his assigned mowing area. Warmed by the rising sun, he removes his red tee shirt and waves it in the air to taunt Pembrook who mows nearby. He loves to insult Pembrook's stuffy sensibilities. He knows that Pembrook can't stand bare-chested mowers.

Zitzelberger sits on the deck buttering his toast. He's about to breakfast on scrambled eggs and two large slabs of bacon. As a hedge against hunger, he has placed a box of Frosted Flakes on the table in case he needs more food to top off the meal. Zitzelberger looks at the cheerful Tony The Tiger on the cereal box. The tiger wears a bright red bandanna around his neck. Zitzelberger reads the caption on the box, and thinks, a*nother **g.r.r.reat!** day in paradise.* He pours a cup of coffee, and glances at his computer display of the property, the only news he cares to see. He looks again in disbelief. *Something's wrong!* All the red rectangles are moving across his computer screen like large insects, except one. Mildly puzzled, he checks the space. It's Finnegan's patch of grass. He can see the area from the deck.

"Gee Whiz!" he says out loud. He had talked to Finnegan before about his tendency to pee in the open. He grabs his binoculars with the idea that he might catch Finnegan in the act of relieving himself. He has few rules, but the acid from urine leaves brown spots in

the grass. Zitzelberger catches Finnegan in his field of vision zigzagging like a madman all over the fairway.

Finnegan's machine moves so fast that he tips over. He tightens his wrestler's grip on the steering wheel, but he's upside down under the skyward-facing wheels. His grass catcher rests on the ground a few yards away like a dead animal. Nearby, a red tee shirt flutters in the wind. He feels the warm trickle of blood on the back of his neck.

Zitzelberger sees Pembrook tripping and slipping while trying to run towards the club house. Pembrook cannot believe his eyes. He thinks, *could this mad scene be a figment of my imagination?* As Pembrook approaches the porch, Zitzelberger hears his shrill voice:

"A wild animal has attacked Finnegan—like a lion or a tiger or a panther of some sort! Finnegan's so hairy the predator likely thought he was a bear. Maybe now people will listen to my suggestions for a dress code. Sure, I could show off my sharply carved torso, too, but mowing half naked is not only ungentlemanly, it's dangerous! I don't know whether Finnegan is dead or alive. Or perhaps somewhere in between...you know, injured. Oh my God, I'm out of breath. I must be close to a cardiacical event. I've sweated my clothes. I need to go back to my house, and change into something more appropriate for witnessing a news making event.

You have no idea how difficult it is to be a fashion icon in a small town!"

***

The cougar rises before first light on Monday morning, resolved to solve the lawnmower noise problem that has climbed to the top of his "to do" list. Although God has equipped him to use lethal force, he has elected, at least for now, to be guided by Shakespeare's Sonnet 94: *"they that have power to hurt but will do none."* The cougar does not need cover. A kill requires cover. A good scare requires visibility. He cat crawls through the swamp to the near edge of the fairway and sees a hairy human yelling and waving a red shirt like he's a matador, the smell of cigar smoke and lawnmower fumes in the air. The cougar breathes in deeply, and produces a baritone roar. *A bit too much vibrato,* he thinks.

He charges, getting up to 45 miles per hour. With the powerful thrust of his hind legs, he leaps for Finnegan, and as planned, grazes the back of Finnegan's neck as he flies over the mower with one long bound. Finnegan opens his mouth to scream, but swallows his cigar instead. Smoke fumes from his mouth and nose like a dragon. He wipes blood from the back of his neck, no more than the blood of a mosquito bite. But when he sees his own blood, he loses control of the mower, tipping it over to face the sky. The lawnmower blades whirr above him until he lets go of the steering wheel to turn off the ignition. Once he swallows the cigar, he howls for help in an authoritative bass. Pembrook runs away from him with soprano alarms. The other mowers look at him shrugging, talking in hushed altos, their flimsy loyalties up for grabs. No one seems to know what's going on.

All together, the cougar thought he had given a well-paced performance, especially with the intricacies of the set, and the eccentricities of the mowers. Despite a lethargic reaction from Custer who would have underreacted to an attack by Sioux warriors, the cougar had fully engaged the rest of the field in a mad fearful romp made up of musical body movement, like Spanish peasants dancing the Bolero in six eight time, connected by fascinating dialogue. He could have solved some of the coordination issues with one or two more cougars, but he had worked well within his limitations. He had scared the hell out of everyone, except Custer who let the whole fiasco pass unnoticed. The cougar felt like a finely tuned predator; like the super being that he happened to be.

From the wood's edge, the cougar sees Zitzelberger walk into the fairway where Finnegan wriggles out from under his mower. Having changed into a new outfit with hunter green pants and high leather boots, Pembrook stumps and shouts at Zitzelberger while waving his leather patched arms. Zitzelberger pays no attention to Pembrook. He pays no attention to Finnegan who might have needed help. He looks straight ahead, shouldering a deer rifle, heading for the tree line on the other side of what used to be the 18th Hole. Custer continues to mow in neat lines as if nothing has happened. The other mowers disappear into the pole barn, and promptly leave the club in a dust cloud of speeding cars and trucks.

Chapter Three
Swallowing the Moon

Zitzelberger returns from his foray to the woods without the cougar's hide. He paces off 150 yards, and staples the Frosted Flakes box to a fence post. He uses Tony the Tiger's big blue nose as a bull's eye for target practice. He raises the gun stock to his cheek and takes dead aim. He fires a three-round pattern into the box, then walks to the target to examine his marksmanship. *"All three hit right in the nose,"* he says to himself. Tony's still smiling on the box cover. Zitzelberger notices the cartoon tiger's human-like finger pointing to the blue sky. *"It's plain silly and against nature to give animals human-like qualities,"* he thinks. The bullet holes look like nostrils on Tony's nose.

The cougar attack threatens Zitzelberger's utopia. The Lawnmower Club shuts down until further notice. He calls the Department of Natural Resources to report a cougar sighting. He's angry. He wants action. The whole situation defies his understanding. God created man to rule over nature and to beat it into submission like an unruly child. That's why you mow a lawn—to keep the grass from getting out of control. That's why you kill animals who threaten your lawn and livelihood. Unnatural acts must be punished.

I spent all my money from the repo business to buy the golf club, and something like this happens! I thought only a few cougars lived in the UP, and didn't bother anyone. Very strange. But I'm not going to let some dumb animal get in the way of my happiness. I'll put an end to this. I'll put an end to him. I've got a business to run. I have to get the mowers back, or I'll be ruined.

Zitzelberger has turned a bankrupt golf course into a personal paradise—his own personal paradise. He has reinvented the world to his own liking. He has turned his imagination into a new reality. The cougar imagines a world before man, and wants the world to be nothing but deep forest. They are both stubborn about what they want. Both unrealistic. What they both want more than anything is to be left alone—to live their lives in their own way.

***

Hearing Zitzelberger's shots, the cougar thinks about death and mortality. *I need to be honest with myself. That was a stupid thing to do...if only the limbic impulses in my brain stem wouldn't be so dominant. If only my hearing wasn't so sensitive. The only solution is to go farther away from people, deeper into the woods. There I would have a better chance to die of natural causes. The world would be a better place without people.*

He edges away from The Lawnmower Club, and fades into the pine shadows. The wind in the trees, and creek water over rocks soothes him. The lawnmower noise lessens to near silence. The cougar sleeps off his worries.

The grass on the fairways grows out of control. Some would say that the grass returns to its natural state. Only Custer continues to mow. Finally, even Custer gives up. In late August, he runs his lawnmower up to a grassy mound, and mows his last patch of grass while wild geese circle.

He stands there thinking about his famous ancestor, *I would like to die like my namesake on a hill like this someday, but not today while not much is going on. I need an audience to die, even if it's hostile. It's in my genes.*

He returns to the cart shed where a sepulchral quiet greets him. Dark and cold inside, the overhead lights flicker yellow. He shuts his mower down, slides the creaky door closed, and wonders why everyone has disappeared.

***

Gloria Fitting knows something's up. Pembrook tells her, "I know this brutal animal attack has happened for a reason, because I keep hearing a voice from outer space telling me to restore the club to its rightful owner...that would be me. The voice may be the word of God...I don't know. Anyway, Zitzelberger must go."

Gloria's snooping activities around Zitzelberger's property remain unabated. The TV weather reporter announces the second full moon of August, a blue moon on the thirty-first—a perfect night for her undercover investigations. She knows that she will prevail over Zitzelberger. Eventually, she will catch him seriously neglecting himself and she will have him committed to Mallard Pond. "I bet he can't even button his shirtsleeves," she smiles.

This evening, she plans to collect samples from his trash bin to document poor eating habits. She'll look for fast food containers, pizza boxes, expired can goods, soda bottles, discarded coupons for fruit and vegetables, and anything else inconsistent with the Mediterranean Diet. She will look for dental floss, the absence of which could indicate poor oral health. And of course, evidence of alcohol and drug abuse—beer cans, liquor, or wine bottles.

In the dark near the ground, she feels strangely serpentine, like a snake has taken possession of her body. Her obsession to control Zitzelberger's life has put her over the edge, or maybe it was her brutal rejection after she auditioned for *The Bachelor*. She loco motes towards the back of the clubhouse with slithering movements, thrusting her body side by side, creating snaky curves in the dirt. She feels like she's in a dream where her anima expresses unfathomable power in the form a large, black snake. The night does strange things to people. For some reason unknown to

Gloria, she slides toward the building, emitting loud hisses.

***

Earlier the same day, Zitzelberger decides to take his shotgun and hunt for rabbits. He thinks gunfire will help keep predators away. He's still sore about the incident. He hasn't seen a soul in days. He misses the mowers, and wants them to come back. As he moves through the remnants of an old apple orchard nearby, a woodcock flushes out of the brush twenty yards in front of him. It's not woodcock season, but Zitzelberger shoots reflexively. The close shot blows the poor bird to smithereens. Zitzelberger gathers what's left of the bird in his large hand, and stuffs the blood, guts, and feathers into the back sleeve pocket of his hunting vest.

After an hour of no rabbits, he returns to the clubhouse. He's hungry from the exercise, and thinks he might pay a rare visit to the local grill for an olive burger. He goes inside to grab his wallet and truck keys. Outside, the night is empty and quiet—only the full moon in the sky. As he turns to exit the clubhouse, Zitzelberger hears a strange sound from his backyard. He looks outside his unhinged back door to see Gloria Fitting on the ground by his trash bin. He recognizes her immediately. She looks like a snake, except for the shrubby bun on the back of her head. He grabs his rifle and runs out. He points the gun at Gloria with an iron gaze. "*All my troubles began with you!*" he says.

He can't believe his opportunity. He has Gloria Fitting under his control. She looks like the child he never wanted. Gloria and the cougar are his main enemies. He might shoot them both, but either way, he would end up in jail. He grabs a length of rope. She looks like hell—curled up and covered with dirt, her loose sweater stained with grass, burrs sticking to her everywhere, her neat bun unraveled, leaving snaky-looking strands of hair. She's frightened; her eyes are bloodshot. The binocular straps hang around her neck like a noose. She knows this could be her doom.

She uncurls and raises up from the ground into a yoga sitting pose; tries to pay attention to her breathing, and avoid distracting thoughts like *I'm going to die soon.* Zitzelberger tells her to stand up. He points to the woods with his gun. She walks before him, wobbling forward silently, already grieving the damage this might cause her career—if she lives. Zitzelberger marches her to the wooded fringe of the 10th Fairway, and ties her to a tree. He wants to leave her over night to give her a good scare. Gloria has scraped herself crawling around in the woods, and the fresh scent of blood fills the moist evening air, not to mention the bloody bird stuck in Zitzelberger's vest. He tightens the rope so she can't escape.

"*Owww, owww...you can't do this to me!*" Gloria says. "*You want a wild animal to kill me. You're going to leave me here to be eaten alive, and all I wanted to do was help you! You won't get away with it. You'll get caught, and then you'll lose your precious club, and even Mallard Pond will reject you—if you don't go to jail. You're making a big mistake, mister. You're old and tired, and your decision-making ability's impaired. I knew something was wrong with your mind!"*

Zitzelberger moves his unkempt head close to hers, and stares at her with the untrimmed hedge of his eyebrows. In the silvery light of the moon, his eyes look like ball bearings. He smiles and turns his back on her. He leaves her in the dark, and slowly stalks towards the clubhouse. Not accustomed to feelings of guilt, Zitzelberger senses a mild discomfort like indigestion.

I'm a really bad man, but I think this may be too much for me. What if the girl gets eaten by the cougar? What if she dies of fright? No, what I did was wrong, wrong, wrong. And besides, I'd never see The Lawnmower Club from the inside of a jail cell. I think I'll return to the clubhouse for a little bite of something, and then go back and let her loose. She'll think I've come to finish her off, but I'll tell her to get off my property, and never come back. She'll be too scared to ever bother me again.

Meanwhile Gloria struggles frantically against the rope until she exhausts herself. *If I get out of this alive, I'm going to get Mr. Zitzelberger into big trouble. I may have nightmares from this. I may need help if I survive. I'm a mess. There's blood on my sweater. I have no budget for dry cleaning. I'll have to see a therapist for sure.*

***

The cougar has difficulty sleeping under the glaring light of the full moon. His long form lays in the grass like a sculptor has cut him from a block of stone. He dreams in fits. He wakes and hears Gloria Fitting crying out for help. He rises to his feet. A human scent is tall in the air with the smell of blood from Gloria's scrapes. The cougar finds her skinny body tied to a tree like a rag doll. She mutters about unresolved issues with her mother. The cougar moves closer and gazes at her with his big cat eyes. Gloria opens her eyes and faints.

This doesn't look like a mower guy, the cougar thinks. She's in enemy territory, but she doesn't look like an enemy. She's too skinny. The cougar's cerebral cortex has not evolved to develop well-defined categories or other high levels of thought, but the girl does not appear to be prey. A tall gun-toting man, on the other hand, falls in the flight or fight region of the cougar's well-developed cerebellum. The cougar sniffs at Gloria for five or six seconds (an eternity for her). Gloria wakes up, feels the cougar's cold nose on her hand, and faints again.

The cougar cocks his head and moves on like he's passing by a bad dish at a progressive dinner. He smells fresh-killed game in the air. The earthy blood of woodcock? He sees Zitzelberger lumbering in a straight line back towards clubhouse, his gun pointed to the ground, his back turned to the cougar. A red plaid hunting cap rests on his head.

The cougar sees feathers and a broken bird leg sticking out of the back of Zitzelberger's vest. The cougar tenses his hind legs as if preparing to leap, which is exactly what he is about to do.

Zitzelberger registers another uncomfortable feeling about tying Gloria to the tree. Even though it's dark, he feels exposed, like he's visible from space. He scratches the back of his neck.

I shouldn't feel bad. I intend to let the girl loose. Why should I feel bad? Sometimes you have to teach people a lesson. After tonight, I'll never see her again. As soon as I have a bit of blueberry muffin in the clubhouse, I'll let her go.

FIGHT RESPONSE!

The cougar loses his peripheral vision. His large green eyes focus on Zitzelberger's back. He becomes all lungs and legs—a killing machine in a fur coat accelerating like a low-flying sports car. He doesn't give Zitzelberger a sporting chance—doesn't circle and face him down or give him a warning growl.

The cougar leaps high into the night air, opening his jaws wide enough to swallow the moon. Zitzelberger's body jitters on the ground. The cougar raises a triumphant howl. Gloria slumps against the tree. Having a bad dream, Pembrook sits up in bed to ward off a vampire cat.

****

ACKNOWLEDGEMENTS

Thanks to my readers who have sustained and supported life as a writer, and who have given me the opportunity to read aloud and receive feedback on my work. Group settings have been especially helpful, including the Bear River Writers Conference, the Charlevoix Writers Group, Friends with Pens, Red Sky Stage, and Wade's Writers.

Thanks to Al Sevener for serving as my steadfast listener and reader, to Wade Rouse (author of The Charm Bracelet by Viola Shipman) for coaching, editing, and moral support, to Mike Schlitt, founder of the Charlevoix Photography Club, for his photographic art, and to Angela Hoy and Todd Engel for their publishing and cover design expertise at BookLocker.

Thanks also to Alison DeCamp (author of My Near-Death Adventure (99% true!)) and Katie Capaldi, Owner, Between the Covers, a bookstore in Harbor Springs, Michigan, for encouraging me, and for reminding me that there is no better place for a new book to debut than on the shelf of an independent bookstore.

And special gratitude goes to Denise Evans, my first reader, cheerleader, critic, and greatest source of sunshine.

ABOUT THE AUTHOR

Randy and Denise Evans live in Bay Harbor, Michigan with Little Traverse Lizzie, their English Setter. Randy graduated from Ohio University, Phi Beta Kappa, in English Literature. He earned an MBA from Columbia University in New York City followed by a career as a human resources executive in manufacturing and high tech industries. After retiring, Randy completed a Ph.D. in psychology at Saybrook University in San Francisco. He teaches developmental psychology at a community college, serves on local boards, and participates in Rotary International. He loves pickleball. Randy invites readers to email him at randenise@yahoo.com or visit randyevansauthor.com.